WOMEN AT THE TOP 2005 CHANGING NUMBERS, CHANGING POLITICS?

Sarah Childs, Joni Lovenduski and Rosie Campbell

HANSARD

Published by the Hansard Society.

40-43 Chancery Lane, London WC2A 1JA

Tel: 020 7438 1222

Fax: 020 7438 1229

Email: hansard@hansard.lse.ac.uk

Website: www.hansardsociety.org.uk

The Hansard Society is an independent, non-partisan educational charity which exists to promote effective parliamentary democracy. For information about other Hansard Society publications visit our web site at www.hansardsociety.org.uk

The views expressed in this publication are those of the authors. The Hansard Society, as an independent, non-party organisation, is neither for nor against the arguments expressed. The Society is, however, happy to publish these views and to invite analysis and discussion.

ISBN: 0 900432 97 7

The Hansard Society is grateful to Accenture for supporting both the 2005 *Women at the Top* Report and accompanying Conference

Production and sub-editing by Virginia Gibbons

Contents

Preface

Fifteen years ago, the Hansard Society Commission on *Women at the Top* drew attention to the 'formidable' barriers - in the form of structures, working practices and, above all, attitudes - preventing women reaching senior positions in the public and private sectors. The Hansard Society has since revisited particular aspects of the original Commission on a five-yearly basis, making this the third update in that series.

It is appropriate, in a general election year, that the co-authors of this latest Report, Dr Sarah Childs, Professor Joni Lovenduski and Dr Rosie Campbell, have chosen to focus on developments in the political sphere. Encouragingly, they outline the progress that has been made. Since 1990, the proportion of women MPs in the House of Commons has more than trebled, now comprising nearly 20 per cent of the total membership, while female representation in the Scottish Parliament and Welsh Assembly is significantly higher: 40 per cent and 50 per cent respectively.

As the Report makes clear, the increased level of women in British political life is due in large part to legislation. The Sex Discrimination (Election Candidates) Act 2002, for example, has made it possible for political parties to take positive action – in the form of All Women Shortlists – to increase female representation. However, not all the political parties have sought to take advantage of this.

The UK Parliament thus still lags significantly behind many other democracies in terms of the number of women in its representative institutions, and is overshadowed by the situation in the devolved assemblies. The principle of justice demands that this inequality be addressed. In the meantime, however, this report acknowledges that those women who have managed to reach 'the top' of politics can still make a difference. Challenging the view that there is a law of 'critical mass', which holds that a certain proportion of women must be present before they can start to substantively change the nature of an institution, the authors argue that women working individually or in small numbers have the ability to make a real impact.

That is a finding which should encourage all women who are active in politics. At the same time, however, it should not be used as an excuse to avoid tackling the inequality of opportunity that keeps the political world overwhelmingly male. As the authors demonstrate, merely using the language of equality, or promoting equality – through special training, or financial assistance – does not guarantee that women will be selected for winnable seats. This is the most persuasive presentation yet of the case that only All Women Shortlists will result in significant and lasting change.

Whether or not one accepts that view, the findings of Women at the Top 2005 should act as a wake-up call to politicians, political parties and everyone concerned to hasten progress towards gender parity in our political institutions. The 'legislative clock' is ticking: in 10 years the special measures enabling parties to take positive action will run out, and if action is not taken well before that, the glass ceiling identified by the Hansard Society Commission back in 1990 will remain firmly in place.

Baroness Howe of Idlicote, CBE
Chair, Hansard Society Commission on Women at the Top, 1990

Foreword

Since the Hansard Society's original *Women at the Top* Commission reported on levels of female representation in public and professional life 15 years ago, the number of women in paid work has grown significantly. Over the same period, the proportion of those in senior levels of leading public and private organisations has also increased. Yet, despite this progress, evidence indicates that inequalities persist and negative attitudes and working practices remain. In consequence, many women are still prevented from fulfilling their potential.

As this investigation into female representation and their impact in political life makes clear, the world of politics is far from immune to such inequality - although at the same time women have made remarkable strides in some areas of the civil service. Indeed, the evidence presented here suggests that women face greater difficulties entering national politics than they do business, the legal profession and many other sectors. So why is that and what does make for success? Inevitably, we have found there is no single recipe. What works in one sector sometimes does not work in another – equally what works for one individual person may not be relevant to another. To drive forward and accelerate the improvements of the last 15 years requires both political and business spheres to develop a climate in which there is both greater demand for, and greater supply of, women capable of operating at top levels.

The Hansard Society Report suggests that this under-representation of women at the top of politics ought to be of special concern, given that those who hold political power can perhaps do the most to tackle the root causes of gender inequality – and serve as an example to society as a whole. Hence, if women are to have an equal chance of success in wider society, it is vital that obstacles in the political sphere are removed.

The Report highlights All Women Shortlists as the quickest and most effective means of delivering equal representation, pointing out that the Labour Party's use of such equality guarantees has been central to the increased number of women in Westminster, the Scottish Parliament and the National Assembly for Wales. Another measure of interest is the Liberal Democrat's use of sex quotas at the shortlisting level, which helps to counter selectorate discrimination. From 2001 to 2005, the number of women MPs from the Liberal Democrats rose 100 per cent - in part a result of these quotas.

In the business sector – whilst it can clearly be seen to be effective in terms of numbers – this overtone of 'positive discrimination' is usually regarded as an anathema. In Accenture our focus is founded on the belief that the best ideas and work are generated from teams rich with diversity of opinion and perspective. The retention and advancement of women is one such example, but equally a focus on ethnic minorities and the disabled would be two other examples. Thus for us, it becomes a focus on achieving the best results through maximising diversity rather than a male vs female debate.

Both public and private sector tend to agree the challenge is to create an environment that:

- Educates, prepares and coaches people from different backgrounds and genders to be able to operate at the top level – often men will require some of the same training as women – sometimes the needs can be gender or culture specific

- Provides a network that allows them to maximise their performance and which is there to support them and to help retain them

- Allows the flexibility and different work approaches which are required to maximise the input from a diverse workforce

Gender bias has been called the last socially acceptable form of discrimination. Accenture has sponsored the *Women at the Top* Report because we are committed to helping women gain as strong a profile as men in both the public and private spheres. Each year we dedicate effort through both internal and external programmes to assist in this goal. We hope this publication, and the accompanying conference to launch its important findings, serves to act as a catalyst for debate about how greater female representation and wider diversity can be achieved in politics, in business and in the civil service – to the overall benefit of the UK.

Lis Astall
UK Managing Director, Accenture

Introduction

This is the fourth Hansard Society Report on *Women at the Top* published in the last 15 years. [1] All of the reports set out to identify and make recommendations regarding the under-representation of women in political and public life. In the past they have examined the numbers of women in Parliament (as MPs and members of the House of Lords), the judiciary, civil service, business, media, trade unions, and the universities. This year's Report, the first written in a general election year, takes a slightly different approach. It focuses in greater depth on women's representation in political life, examining the feminisation of politics: the integration of women and women's concerns *and* perspectives in British politics.

The Report has three aims:

1 To identify the causes of women's under-representation in British politics

2 To make recommendations to improve the representation of women in the UK's elected political institutions, and

3 To address women's substantive representation (the representation of women's concerns and perspectives). It uses the 2005 general election as a case study, although it also draws upon previous Westminster elections and examples from the devolved institutions and other international cases.

The narrower focus in the 2005 Report reflects an emergent consensus that the level of women's representation in UK political institutions is determined less by 'supply-side' factors, such as women's educational, occupational or economic resources than by 'demand-side' factors, not least discrimination by those who select candidates for political office. Such conclusions suggest earlier optimism that women's representation will inevitably increase significantly over time as their presence in the roles and occupations characteristic of male politicians increases is misplaced, and that recommendations to enhance women's numerical representation are similarly likely to be of a political, rather than socio-economic or cultural nature. Consequently, the Report looks in much greater detail than previous reports at the selection processes for Parliament of the main political parties, not least in outlining and evaluating the ways in which, given their shared public commitments to increasing the numbers of women elected to the House of Commons, each has made substantial revisions to their selection procedures.

The considerable space devoted to answering questions of whether women make a difference to politics and how women's presence in Parliament (descriptive representation) engenders the representation of women's concerns (substantive representation) differentiates this Report from previous ones. In the past, this question has only been discussed in passing. In the 1990 Commission Report it was stated that 'the relative paucity of women MPs may mean that the interests of women are not properly represented in Parliament, on Select Committees, or in Government' (Hansard Society 1990, 29); while in the 2000 Report the question of whether the greater numbers of women MPs in the 1997 Parliament had 'made a difference' was raised but not answered, not least because of a lack of available data. Some eight years on from that election, and with the new devolved institutions also returning high numbers of women members, sufficient time has passed for more systematic analysis to be presented.

The 2005 *Women at the Top* Report is divided into three sections. The first begins by briefly updating the previous reports before considering in detail the political recruitment of women MPs at the 2005 general election and comparing this with women's representation in the devolved institutions. The second explores the question of whether the entrance of women into politics has the related effect of bringing women's concerns and perspectives into politics. A number of case studies, drawn from Westminster, the Scottish Parliament and the National Assembly for Wales, are presented to demonstrate that there is evidence of feminised change. The third section provides international comparison with discussions of political recruitment practices elsewhere, not least the use of sex quotas, and further case studies of women effecting a feminisation of politics. The Report closes with a list of recommendations. These include, but are not limited to, the use by all political parties of equality guarantees, permitted under the 2002 Sex Discrimination (Election Candidates) Act, to ensure that higher proportions of women are selected as candidates for winnable seats and thereby elected to the UK's political institutions.

The first *Women at the Top* Report, published in 1990, reported the findings of a Hansard Society Commission that was established to consider the 'under-representation of women in the upper reaches of public life in this country, and in particular in the House of Commons', a situation which the then Chair of the Hansard Society considered a 'serious anomaly' (Hansard Society 1990, vii). In particular, the Commission, chaired by Lady Howe, was to identify 'barriers to the appointment of women to senior occupational positions, and to other positions of power and influence, and to make recommendations as to how these barriers could be overcome' (Hansard Society 1990, viii). The Commission's final Report reflected this broad approach by assessing the problems facing women at the top of public, corporate and professional life - 'from which the leadership of the country is drawn' – and identifying emerging solutions to these problems as well as offering examples of good practice (Hansard Society 1990, xiv). It identified key barriers to women's equality: outdated attitudes about the role of women; direct and indirect discrimination; the absence of proper child-care provision; and inflexible structures for work and careers (Hansard Society 1990, 2). With respect to women's under-representation in Parliament, the Report noted that Westminster was 'almost at the bot-tom of the league table of modern democracies', and recommended that:

> ... a Speaker's Conference be established to consider the ways in which parliamentary and party practices and procedures place women at a disadvantage...and that the political parties should scrutinise their own policies and practices, and eliminate those that serve to hinder the progress of women' (Hansard Society 1990, 4).

The second Women at the Top Report, published in 1996 set out to establish whether the earlier recommendations had been acted upon and to what effect.[2] Its evaluation of women's representation in Parliament reiterated the importance of 'family-friendly' working practices, acknowl-edging that such practices would 'make it easier for women with chil-dren to work as Members of Parliament' - portentously adding the qual-ification 'provided, of course, that they are elected' (Hansard Society 1996, 7, emphasis added). In this respect the Report documented the failure of the Conservative Party to select women in its winnable seats and noted the use of All Women Shortlists (AWS) by the Labour Party in its winnable seats (Hansard Society 1996, 18). It projected a tripling in the number of Labour women MPs at the 1997 election, although it acknowledged that the policy of AWS had already been abandoned. (A full discussion of the use of AWS is provided later in Section 1.)

In light of the record numbers of women elected to Parliament in 1997 and the devolved institutions in 1999, the third Report concluded that:

> ...*without determined measures which actually force parties to widen participation to include women and for them to be allocated to winnable seats, Parliaments and Assemblies will continue to be dominated by men, not because they are better than women but because selection processes make it difficult for women to secure nominations (Hansard Society 2000, 4).*

It recommended the use of 'specific acts of will, positive action strategies and a strong steer from government and other policy makers' (Hansard Society 2000, 24).

The particular focus upon women's political representation in the 2005 Report is not intended to suggest that analysis of women's presence in other areas of public life and the professions is not, in itself, important nor that lessons cannot be learnt from equal opportunities good practice in these areas. Advocates of women's equal political participation should be concerned about the numbers and characteristics of women who are present in public life or who succeed in the professions, in themselves - not least for what they tell us about the re-gendering of the public and private spheres and, in particular, the extent to which women are constrained by traditional gender roles and responsibilities and/or experience sex discrimination.

Our summary, which updates the findings of previous *Women at the Top* Reports (see Appendix 1), suggests that in most areas since the 2000 Report, there has been only incremental improvement in the representation of women. Women are still dramatically under-represented in key areas of public, political and economic life: the majority of public appointments, senior civil servants, members of the legal profession, directors of FTSE 100 companies, key actors in the media and individuals holding senior positions in our universities, are men - usually white men.

Moreover, recent high profile reports confirm that women's paid employment patterns continue to be characterised by horizontal segregation (the sticky floor and glass ceiling) and vertical segregation (glass partitions) as well as part time work. [3] This leaves many women concentrated in the low paid sectors of caring, cleaning, catering, cashiering and clerical work – the five 'C's – working disproportionately in the public rather than private sector (64 per cent compared with 41 per cent, respectively) and close to their homes to accommodate their domestic responsibilities (EOC 2005). In addition, and despite the recent extension of maternity and paternity provision, there is extensive maternity discrimination in the UK: almost half of all pregnant women experience some form of disadvantage at work, with some 30,000 forced out of their jobs (EOC 2005).

Together, the features of women's paid and unpaid employment have given rise to a gender pay gap in the UK that is one of the worst in Europe (Bellamy and Rake 2005): women working full-time earn only 82 per cent of the hourly wage of men working full-time whilst women part-time workers (almost half of the women in paid employment) earn 59 per cent of men's full-time hourly pay (Women and Work Commission 2005). [4] Furthermore, women constitute the elderly poor: one in five single women pensioners lives in poverty, only 13 per cent have entitlement to a full state pension and 30 per cent to a private pension in their own right. [5]

Achieving gender equality in paid employment requires, *inter alia*, reform to women's education, particularly at the vocational level; a commitment to women's life-long learning, particularly for returning mothers; an end to employment segregation and pay inequalities; and greater efforts to guarantee an acceptable work-life balance with rights to flexible working and more extensive maternity provision and child-care (EOC 2002). Yet, with women's experience of paid work diverse rather than uniform - educated women who are childless or have fewer children in later life experience better paid employment than women with lower levels of education, greater caring responsibilities and par-ticular groups of Black and Minority Ethnic (BME) women – there is a need to recognise the particular experiences of different groups, as well as the more general issue of women's continuing disproportionate responsibility for the private sphere which limits and disadvantages individual women's participation (Bellamy and Rake 2005).

The focus on women's political representation in the 2005 Report should also not be taken to imply that the representation of women in public life and the professions or the characteristics of women's paid and unpaid employment more generally, do not impact on or cannot influence women's numerical representation in politics. Without sug-gesting that women representatives will only (or more problematically, *should* only) be women with professional backgrounds, greater num-bers and a greater diversity of women in the professions and public life is a 'good thing' for women's political representation. In part this will be symbolic – greater numbers and different kinds of women heading up FTSE 100 companies, running our universities, and making our laws, should act to normalise women's presence in places where they have previously been absent or under-represented. It may also have a more direct impact, with more women gaining the resources and motivation to undertake political participation and seek political office. However, the assumption that women entering into professional and public life in greater numbers will somehow, and automatically, translate into significantly greater numbers of women in our political institutions has, over the last 20 years, been proven wrong. It assumes that the under-representation of women in politics is predominantly a problem of a lack of supply of women seeking political office – when, in fact, even when the political parties have selected women candidates in greater numbers it is too often for contests they simply cannot win.

Neither is it to say that political parties cannot learn from the equal opportunities good practices of the public sphere. Indeed, they may be an important factor in expanding the numbers of women in the political supply pool: as parties signal their demand for women candidates through employing equal opportunities measures, more women may be encouraged to seek selection. Equal opportunities practices are also likely to be necessary to retain women once they have been elected to political institutions – by providing, for example, generous maternity leave, establishing family friendly working practices and allowing flexible working patterns. However, in and of themselves, equal opportunities practices are limited in delivering the election of greater numbers of women politicians. Where significant gains have been made in British politics, whether that is at the 1997 general election or the elections to the Scottish Parliament or National Assembly for Wales in 1999, the overriding explanation points to the use by (some) political parties of equality guarantees – measures that require a particular number or proportion of women to be elected. This suggests that, in contrast to the reasoning behind the earlier *Women at the Top* Reports' broad focus – the assumption that women's success in public life was likely to be preceded and complemented by their achievements in wider society (Hansard Society 1990, xiii) - the barriers to women's greater political participation in the UK have more to do with the workings of politics *per se*, than wider societal or structural features.

[1] We would like to thank the Hansard Society, and in particular Declan McHugh, Gemma Rosenblatt and Vidya Ram for their advice and support in the writing of this Report and to Gemma especially for her research on women in public life and the professions. We would also like to thank Trish Morris and Andrew Whitby-Collins at the Conservative Party, Peter Watt at the Labour Party, and Karen Gillard at the Liberal Democrats for providing us with information about their selection procedures for the 2005 general election. Finally, we would like to thank Dr Rob Dover for his comments on the draft introduction and Drs. Paul Chaney and Fiona Mackay (the Universities of Cardiff and Edinburgh, respectively), for so generously allowing us to draw on their, as yet unpublished, research findings on the Scottish Parliament and National Assembly for Wales. We are, furthermore, grateful to the Nuffield Foundation for funding the BRS 2005 (SGS/01180/G) and to Accenture for supporting the 2005 *Women at the Top* Report and accompanying Conference.

[2] The Report states that 'by convention' Speaker's Conferences deal with aspects of electoral law and not with the internal workings of Parliament (Hansard Society 1996, 7).

[3] *The Economist* 4 June 2005 'Sex Changes'. Forty-five per cent of women work part-time compared to 10 per cent of men.

[4] Working in the public sector reduces the full-time gender pay gap, - the full-time gender pay gap is 10.1 per cent in the public but 21.3 per cent in the private sector - but not the part-time gender pay gap, which is the same in both sectors.

[5] www.ePolitix.com: 'London's women face biggest pay gap' (11 Jan 2005).

SECTION 1

The Political Recruitment of Women in British Politics

If Margaret Thatcher proves to be a successful Prime Minister, perhaps 10-15 years from now an influx of young women taking their cue from her achievements may be permitted to flow into the political elite. As always political change in Britain moves with glacial speed (Rasmussen 1981, 620)

Comparing the House of Commons in 2005 with the 1987 Parliament (the time of the original *Women at the Top* Commission) establishes a three-fold increase in the numbers of women MPs elected (see Table 1). Of the 646 MPs elected in 2005, 128 were women. [6] In 1987 there had been just 41. Comparing recent general election results with the post-war period more generally, the increases since the late 1990s appear to have been far from glacial: after four decades where women's representation averaged around three to four per cent, in the space of three elections, a step-change at nearer 20 per cent seems to have been established.

TABLE 1: No.s OF WOMEN MPs ELECTED TO THE HOUSE OF COMMONS 1945-2005

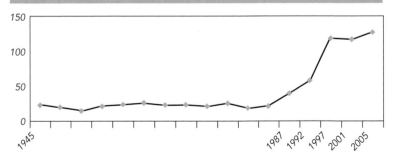

The upward trend of women's political representation at the 2005 general election masks a more complex story of the numerical representation at Westminster, and more generally in the UK. The election of 128 women MPs in 2005 was indeed a welcome increase on the previous general election which had seen the first fall in a generation in the numbers of women MPs returned - from the 1997 high of 120 to 118 in 2001. But the improvements in 2005 were, just as in 2001 and 1997, party specific and dependent upon the use of equality guarantees: not only are women MPs disproportionately from the Labour Party, more than half of all Labour women MPs currently sitting in Parliament were selected on All Women Shortlists (AWS) in 1997 or 2005. It is not so much, then, that women *en masse* have been *permitted* entrance to the UK House of Commons but rather that one political party (Labour) has introduced measures that *forced* their entry.

TABLE 2: MPs ELECTED TO THE HOUSE OF COMMONS, 1983-2005 [7]						
Party	**1983**	**1987**	**1992**	**1997**	**2001**	**2005**
Labour	209	229	271	418	412	354
Women	10	21	37	101	95	98 [8]
% of Total	**4.8**	**9.2**	**13.7**	**24.2**	**23.1**	**27.7**
Conservative	397	376	336	165	166	198
Women	13	17	20	13	14	17
% of Total	**3.3**	**4.5**	**6**	**7.9**	**8.4**	**8.6**
Liberal Democrat	23	22	20	46	53	62
Women	0	1	2	3	6 [9]	10 [10]
% of Total	**0**	**4.5**	**10**	**6.5**	**11.3**	**16.1**
Other	21	23	24	30	25	31
Women	0	2	3	3	4	3
% of Total	**0**	**8.7**	**12.5**	**10**	**16**	**9.7**
All MPs	650	650	651	659	659	645
Women	23	41	60	120	118	128
% of Total	**3.5**	**6.3**	**9.2**	**18.2**	**17.9**	**19.8** [11]

A second aspect of the 2005 general election that is often missed is the internationally comparatively low numerical representation of women in Parliament. Although a few points above the 16 per cent global average of women's representation, the House of Commons ranks 47th in the Inter Parliamentary Union league table (http://www.ipu.org/wmn-e/classif.htm, Sept 2005), below *inter alia*, Rwanda (in first place), the Nordic countries, Holland, Spain, Argentina, South Africa and Germany. Closer to home, it compares unfavourably with the Scottish Parliament and the National Assembly for Wales, where women represent 40 and 50 per cent respectively (see Table 3 below). Furthermore, these unflattering comparisons question the explanatory value of previously identified factors said to account for women's low levels of numerical representation.

TABLE 3: WOMEN'S NUMERICAL REPRESENTATION IN UK POLITICS

Institution	Percentage of Women
National Assembly for Wales	50
Scottish Parliament	40
GLA	36
European Parliament	24
Westminster	20
Northern Ireland Assembly	17

Finally, an optimistic reading of the 2005 general election fails to consider what the representation of women should be, normatively speaking. It is often said (by the UN for example) that women should constitute at least 30 per cent of the representatives in our political institutions. However, there has been a recent shift in the discourse of women's representation, away from 'greater representation' towards 'parity', the equal representation of women and men (Lovenduski 2005). Achieving parity in the UK Parliament looks to be a long way off, not least because achieving a female membership of 30 per cent (itself an arbitrary figure) appears to lie beyond the horizon for all parties other than Labour. Moreover, any discussion about women's political representation must acknowledge the question of diversity: BME women are particularly under-represented in politics – as are BME men.

Explaining Women's Political Recruitment

The under-representation of women in politics is a global phenomenon: there are no cases of national parliaments where women are equally represented (the National Assembly for Wales, which does not have primary legislative powers, aside). Neither is there, as might be assumed, a linear relationship between countries' economic or social development and the levels of women's political representation. Cross-national comparisons reveal that countries with widely differing economic, social and political structures and cultures can have similar percentages of women present in their political institutions. The higher percentages of women elected in the Nordic countries might conform to expectations – not least because of their history of social democracy and use of proportional systems of election. But what of the relatively low rankings of other advanced industrial nations such as the UK and the US? Or the African and Latin American countries which make it into the global top 20? There is, in short, no single explanation for women's political representation that holds for all time and all places. Socio-economic, cultural and political determinants of women's numerical representation combine in many different ways to account for the level of elected women in a particular legislature at a particular moment (Further discussion of the global situation is contained in Section 3).

Previous Hansard Society Reports have noted that the determinants of women's representation in the UK include women's traditional gender roles (women are socialised 'to put themselves last'), the inflexibility of

Parliament (by which they mean the incompatibility between women's domestic and parliamentary responsibilities), sex discrimination by party 'selectorates' (those within parties who choose candidates) who contend that women candidates are vote losers or do not have the appropriate background to be politicians, and the preference under Westminster's 'first past the post' electoral system to favour typical, that is, male candidates.

Norris and Lovenduski (1995), in their study of political recruitment in the UK, identify four levels of analysis. At the first level are *systemic* factors that set the broad context within any country: the legal, electoral, party systems and the structure of party competition, the strength of parties and the position of the parties across the ideological divide. The second level looks towards the *context* within parties – their organisation, rules and ideology. At the third level are the *individual* factors such as resources and motivations of aspirant candidates and the attitudes of the party selectorates. Finally, there are the individual *elections* that determine the outcome of the process for the composition of parliaments.

In the UK systemic factors are not significant inhibitors of women's representation. Women do not face legal barriers to their election, although our majoritarian electoral system is widely considered to be less favourable than proportional representation systems, as the first Hansard Society Report acknowledged. Furthermore, in party democracies like the UK, where the overwhelming majority of MPs are representatives of political parties, the question of who our representatives are is one of whom our political parties select as their candidates. Their choice is, in turn, determined by the parties' internal organisation, the nature of their selection processes and their wider beliefs about the role of women and men in public life. If political parties are institutionally sexist – dominated by one sex in terms of its personnel, outcome and practice – this will negatively impact on the selection of women candidates (Lovenduski 2005).

The outcome of parties' selection processes is often understood in terms of the interaction between the *supply* of applicants wishing to pursue a political career and the *demands* of selectors who choose candidates on the basis of their preferences and perceptions of abilities, qualifications and perceived electability (Norris and Lovenduski 1995). Supply-side factors identified as likely to limit the overall level of women seeking selection below their proportionate presence in the population, include gendered socialisation and the sexual division of labour. These cause women to have, on average, fewer resources than men – whether that is the necessary free time to engage in politics, money to fund a selection and election campaign, and/or lower levels of political ambition and confidence. On the demand side, women have been found to suffer from selectorate discrimination (see Box 1), with party selectorates preferring candidates with resources primarily associated with men and masculinity (Norris and Lovenduski 1995; Shepherd-Robinson and Lovenduski 2002). As interviews with women seeking candidatures for the 2001 general election revealed, women faced overt and indirect discrimination. One aspiring female candidate was told, 'well you didn't do bad for a little woman, did you?' while another woman reported the following comment: 'we do enjoy watching you speak, we always imagine what your knickers are like' (Shepherd-Robinson and Lovenduski 2002, 1213). [12]

BOX 1: SELECTORATE DISCRIMINATION

Direct Discrimination	**Indirect Discrimination**
Where gender discriminatory questions are posed to women during the selection processes	Where ideas of what constitutes a good MP have counted against women

Strategies to increase the representation of women

There are three available strategies open for political parties who wish to increase the numbers of women representatives, and indeed the diversity of their representatives more generally: equality *rhetoric*, equality *promotion* and equality *guarantees* (see Box 2) (Lovenduski 2005).

BOX 2: STRATEGIES TO INCREASE THE DIVERSITY OF CANDIDATES

Type of strategy	Definition	Examples	Impact
Equality rhetoric	Public acceptance of claims for representation	Found in party campaign platforms; party political discourse; speeches and writings of political leaders (exhortation of women to come forward and seek selection)	Affects selectorate and aspirant candidates' attitudes and beliefs
Equality promotion	Attempts to bring those who are currently under-represented into political competition	Special training; financial assistance; the setting of targets	Enhances aspirant candidates' resources and motivation; affects selectorate attitudes
Equality guarantees	Requires an increase in the number or proportion of particular candidates; makes a particular social characteristic a necessary qualification for office	Party quotas, legislative quotas; reserved seats	Creates an artificial demand; may increase supply

If supply-side explanations of women's political representation are paramount, equality rhetoric and promotion should deliver greater numbers of women representatives, at least for those women who have the necessary resources to participate. Whereas if demand is the problem, neither equality rhetoric nor equality promotion are likely to be of great effect: equality rhetoric may encourage greater numbers of women to enter the candidate recruitment pool and equality promotion may ensure that women aspirant candidates are sufficiently better prepared, trained, and resourced. But neither of these is sufficient to guarantee that party selectorates will choose women for winnable seats. Indeed, Labour's and the Liberal Democrat's use of sex quotas on their shortlists for the 2001 general election singularly failed to deliver the election of greater numbers of women MPs (see Table 2 above); Conservative Party exhortation has similarly had little effect. In short, to ensure that selectorate discrimination plays no role in the recruitment process, equality guarantees – the creation of an artificial demand by political parties – are necessary.

BOX 3: DIFFERENT QUOTA SYSTEMS

Quota Type	Definition	Illustrative Examples
Constitutional Quota for National Parliament	Quota provisions that are mandated in the constitution of the country	Burkina Faso, Nepal, the Philippines and Uganda
Election Law Quota or Regulation for National Parliament	Quotas that are provided for in the national legislation or regulations of the country	Latin American, Belgium, Bosnia Herzegovina and Sudan
Political Party Quota for Electoral Candidates	Rules or targets set by political parties to include a certain percentage of women as election candidates	Argentina, Bolivia, Ecuador, Germany, Norway, Italy, Sweden, South Africa, UK

Source: http://www.quotaproject.org/system.cfm#constnational

The relative importance of supply- and demand-side explanations for women's legislative recruitment for Westminster (and therefore the relative merits of equality rhetoric, promotion and guarantees) has varied over time and between the political parties. Historically, it was said that the problem was one of supply, with the consequent assumption that if only more women put themselves forward as candidates more would be selected, and in turn, elected. However, by the 1990s supply had become less of a problem for the Labour Party (Shepherd-Robinson and Lovenduski 2002) and at the 2005 general election the three main parties selected over 400 women as parliamentary candidates, although, in no case did women constitute 30 per cent of all candidates. Yet, with between 118-166 women candidates each, all three main parties had more than enough women to fill half their vacancies with women; that is, the seats they already held where the sitting MP was retiring and/or half their target seats. So absolute numbers of candidates is not really the issue; what is, is the selection of women candidates for each party's winnable seats.[13]

TABLE 4: WOMEN CANDIDATES FOR THE MAIN PARTIES, 1992-2005			
	Conservative	**Labour**	**Liberal Democrat**
1992	63	138	143
1997	69	157	140
2001	92	146	135
2005	118	166	142

Sources: P. Norris and J. Lovenduski (1995) *Political Recruitment* Cambridge University Press and *The British Parliamentary Constituency Database, 1992-2005.*

Equality Guarantees in the UK:
The Sex Discrimination (Election Candidates) Act, 2002

The opportunity to employ equality guarantees at the 2005 general election was available to all political parties following the Sex Discrimination (Election Candidates) Act 2002, which introduced a new section (42A) to the Sex Discrimination Act (SDA). This dis-applies the anti-discrimination rules in Parts 2 to 4 of the Act from arrangements which 'regulate the selection by a political party registered under the Political Parties, Elections and Referendums Act 2000 of candidates in an election for Parliament' *and* 'are adopted for the purpose of reducing the inequality in the numbers of men and women elected, as candidates of that party, to be members of the body concerned'. The Act's remit includes elections for Westminster, the European Parliament, the Scottish Parliament and National Assembly for Wales and local government elections. Because the Act permits, but does not prescribe, the use of equality guarantees (see Box 4), it was up to the individual political parties to decide whether to take up the opportunities offered by the new legislation for the 2005 general election.

BOX 4: DIFFERENT TYPES OF QUOTAS		
Equality Guarantees	**Definition**	**Illustrative Examples**
All Women Shortlists (AWS)	A certain percentage of local constituency parties must select their candidate from a list made up only of women aspirant candidates	British Labour Party for the1997 and 2005 general elections. Labour Party Wales 2003.
Twinning	Constituencies are 'paired'; one male and one female candidate is selected for the twinned constituencies	Labour Party for the Scottish and Welsh elections in 1999
Zipping	Men and women are placed alternately on the list of candidates	Liberal Democrats for the 1999 European elections
Reserved Seats	A percentage of seats are formally reserved for women	Bangladesh, Botswana, Pakistan, Taiwan, and Tanzania

Source: Amended from Lovenduski (2005)

The history of the new Act lies in the Labour Party's adoption (in 1993) of, and then the industrial tribunal ruling against, All Women Shortlists (AWS) in the run up to the 1997 general election.[14] The party had first accepted the principle of sex quotas in 1986. But it failed to implement its commitment to secure 50 per cent of women in the Parliamentary Labour Party (PLP) within 10 years or three general elections, by using sex quotas at the 1992 general election. For the 1997 general election the party committed itself to introduce AWS in half of its key seats (winnable on a six per cent swing) and in half of all vacant Labour held seats (Childs 2004; Lovenduski 2005).

At the time of the industrial tribunal ruling in 1996, AWS were having their desired effect: 35 women candidates had already been selected on them. Yet, despite previously having been advised that candidate selection was exempt from the Sex Discrimination Act and although it set no precedent, Labour accepted the industrial tribunal ruling against the party; AWS were stopped and, in an uncertain legal context – that is, in the absence of the Labour government introducing new legisla- tion permitting positive discrimination - there was to be no return to such measures for the 2001 general election.

However, in the context of a decline in the numbers of women MPs elected at the 2001 general election, Labour women MPs campaigning within their party, and extra-parliamentary pressure from women's organisations to act, Tony Blair, despite his earlier antipathy to AWS, agreed to the introduction of the Sex Discrimination (Election Candidates) Act (Childs 2002; 2003). The Bill was easily passed, notwithstanding parliamentary concerns about its compatibility with EU law, the European Convention on Human Rights and international human rights law (Russell 2000; 2001): there was cross-party frontbench support for the principle of the legislation in the Commons' and Lords' debates. Not one MP or Peer argued that women should not be present in greater numbers in the House of Commons. [16] Nonetheless, supporting the Act as it made its way through Parliament is not the same thing as supporting specific measures to implement the principle behind the legislation. As suggested above, the Act's permissive nature means that unless each of the political parties takes up the opportunities it provides then there will be, as likely, no significant change in the number of women MPs elected. This proved to be the case. At the 2005 general election only Labour chose to introduce equality guarantees; other parties' support - however welcome it might have been during the Parliamentary debates – proved ultimately to be rhetorical.

Party selection procedures for the 2005 General Election

The selection practices of all the political parties involve broadly similar stages: of approval, application, nomination, shortlisting and selection. Equality rhetoric, promotion and guarantees are evident in some but not all of the political parties at these different stages, as Table 5 shows.

TABLE 5: USE OF EQUALITY STRATEGIES 2005 GENERAL ELECTION BY PARTY			
	Conservative	**Labour**	**Lib Dem**
Equality Rhetoric	Exhortation	Exhortation	Exhortation
Equality Promotion	Incorporation of non-sexist selection criteria for approved list	Incorporation of non-sexist selection criteria for approved list	Incorporation of non-sexist selection criteria for approved list
	Training of some selectors in fair practices	Training of selectors in fair practices	Training of some selectors in fair practices
	Training for approved candidates - some women only	Training for approved candidates	One-third sex-quota at shortlisting stage
	Primaries and CSI	Units nominate one man and one woman	
		Parity sex quota at shortlisting stage [17]	
Equality Guarantees		AWS	

Labour Party

The Labour Party used all three equality strategies to increase the numbers of women selected and elected to Parliament in 2005. Equality rhetoric and promotion operated at the preparation, application and shortlisting stages of Labour's selection procedures and the Party used AWS (equality guarantees) in 30 constituencies.

Committed in the longer term to 50:50 representation of women and men, the Labour Party set its immediate sights on securing 35 per cent women MPs at the 2005 general election. To achieve this, the Party acknowledged, would require the selection of women in those seats it already held – it was most unlikely that, seeking a third term, Labour would win any new seats. Sitting Labour MPs were, therefore, asked to inform the Party of their intention to stand down at the 2005 general election before December 2002. [18] If too few of these constituencies volunteered to be AWS then the National Executive of the party (NEC) would impose them in 50 per cent of vacant seats. All post-December 2002 retirements would be classified as 'late retirements' and automatically declared an AWS, although the NEC retained the power to authorise exceptions in special circumstances (*Guardian* 10 and 29 January 2003).

In addition to seeking greater numbers of women MPs, the Party was simultaneously trying to avoid the perception that 'no men need apply' and seeking to increase the numbers of BME candidates and MPs. The former goal ensured that the percentage of AWS would, in reality, be fewer than 50 per cent; the latter goal meant that seats deemed by the party to be winnable by a BME candidate, namely, where the constituency had a significant BME population, were less likely to be classified as an AWS.

Labour also relied upon general exhortation by Party leaders, in its literature, and sex- specific exhortation by associated organisations such as Labour Women's Network. There were also specific measures aimed at promoting women's candidacies: at the nomination stage Party Units are asked to submit nominations for a man and a woman while affiliated organisations were similarly 'entitled' 'to nominate both a man and a woman' *(Labour's Future* 39-40). At the shortlisting stage the Labour Party has a sex balancing rule: 'if four or more are nominated there shall be a minimum of FOUR in any shortlist (ie at least TWO men and TWO women)' (emphasis in the original, *Labour's Future,* 75).

Furthermore, the Party's literature on candidate selection *(Labour's Future* and the *NPP Application Pack)* stresses the importance of quality and diversity of candidates; that the process of selection must ensure equality of opportunity and that 'Labour's candidates are drawn from the widest possible pool of talent'. It reminds members that they should avoid 'making assumptions based on physical characteristics, dress, body language or voice'. The guidelines also emphasise that candidates with caring responsibilities 'may not have work-related or trade union experience, but may be active in the community'. Candidates should also be judged in respect of their commitment to equal opportunities: 'work which candidates have been involved in could focus on race, gender, disability, sexuality, economic equality, or any work which increases the opportunity or influence of under-represented or disadvantaged groups in society. Proscribed questions that cannot be asked at the hustings meetings include those of a sexist nature and those that enquire into a candidate's marital state or domestic circumstances *(Labour's Future,* 13).[19]

Moreover, for Labour Party members participating in the selection vote, the following declaration must be signed:

> I am aware that in casting my vote in this selection procedure I must vote for a candidate purely on the basis of merit. I will not allow the gender of a candidate or any consideration that might favour one gender over another to affect my judgement (Labour's Future, 60). [20]

The Conservative Party

Opposed to equality guarantees on the basis that such measures offend principles of meritocracy, the Conservative Party in 2005 preferred to use equality rhetoric and promotion measures to increase the numbers of its women candidates. Successful attendance at a Parliamentary Assessment Board (PAB) is the first hurdle that aspirant candidates must pass in order to make it onto the Party's Approved List. [21] Informed by equal opportunities good practice, the PABs, this time around, assessed six core competencies and the party was confident that it had created a level playing field:

1 Communication skills (listening as well as speech making)
2 Intellectual skills (taken on board/distil complex information)
3 Relating to (different kinds of) people
4 Leadership and motivation (enthusing, supporting, enabling)
5 Resilience and drive (avoiding arrogance)
6 Conviction (to conservative ideas and commitment to public service)

Once on the Approved List, women, especially those in target seats, would receive training, some of which was 'women only'.

Turning to the selection stages, important changes for the 2005 general election devised to enhance the diversity of Conservative Party candidates included: the removal of education from CVs, to avoid decisions based on attendance at the *'right* school or university'; [22] the encouragement of the constituency 'paper sift' of applications to be undertaken in London so that this could be overseen to ensure there was 'nobody languishing' in the 'no' pile who 'shouldn't be' there; and the invitation to non-party members in local constituencies (recruitment experts, in particular) to participate, although not vote, in the selection process.

More dramatically, the party introduced American-style 'primaries' and the 'city seats strategy' (CSI). Both of these approaches can be regarded as efforts by the centre to introduce measures, albeit ones short of equality guarantees, which would encourage the selection of greater numbers of women (and BME candidates). In respect of the former, the selectorate is effectively extended beyond members of the local association. Although members of the local association continue to determine the shortlist from which the final selection is made, and endorse, through a special general meeting, the chosen candidate. In respect of the latter, part of a wider strategy to revive the Party's fortunes in the inner cities, teams of would-be MPs would be brought together, with the assistance of Party HQ, to campaign city-wide. Only close to the election would individual candidates be 'slotted' into particular seats, although, to counteract local resistance local parties were given the opportunity to reject individual candidates as members of their city team.

BOX 5: PRIMARIES	
Open	Selection is open to anyone who wants to register to be involved
Closed	Selection is limited to all who have registered as a Conservative [23]

Liberal Democrats

The Liberal Democrat Party, just like the Conservatives, chose not to employ equality guarantees permitted by the Sex Discrimination (EC) Act. The issue of equality guarantees publicly divides the Party – their 2001 Conference opposed quotas and young liberal women wore pink T-shirts bearing the slogan *I am not a token woman*, whilst Charles Kennedy has been persuaded of their merits, as he admitted on BBC's *Woman's Hour* in February 2005.

As in the other parties, all applicants seeking parliamentary candidature for the Liberal Democrats must be on an official approved list – a process that involves a standard application form and attendance at a 'Development Day'. The exercises assessed at the Development Day were devised so that the assessment procedure 'can be seen to be fair to all candidates and to the Party'. Moreover, the Party's 'guidance notes for candidates' is sensitive to gender differences. For example, 'domestic' is included as an occupational category while in the section on motivations, qualities and goals, it is suggested that 'planning a big wedding' might constitute an example of strategic planning.

In terms of the constituency selection, the Party's returning officers must have undergone training in selection procedures and the operation of 'selection committees' must ensure 'fair and equal treatment of all candidates'. Similarly, the selection committee should be balanced in terms of sex and, in target and party-held seats, all members, (and in other seats at least two members) 'must' have received the Party's training, 'especially as regards conducting interviews and ensuring equal treatment of applicants'. In addition, non-trained members should be made 'aware of the purpose of shortlisting and their responsibilities as regards equal opportunities and fairness'. Furthermore two equal opportunity forms, 'Selection Committee Forms I and II', 'monitor whether particular groups of candidates are finding it more difficult to get through the selection procedures successfully'.

At the shortlisting stage the Liberal Democrats also operate a one-third sex balancing rule:

> *Subject to there being a sufficient number of applicants of each sex, shortlists of three or four must include at least one member of each sex, and shortlists of five or six must include at least two members of each sex*

According to the returning officers' training pack:

> *Once the scores [of the constituency specific selection criteria] have been added up by the RO, the candidates for each gender should be ranked in order. ...taking into account gender balance, the top, 3, 4, 5, or 6, candidates should make up the list. No candidate on the list should have scored less than an excluded candidate of the same gender, unless that candidate failed to score enough against an essential criteria. The selection committee needs to take this approach on board, before they start marking. The possibility of altering the rankings after the marks have been added up is very limited and hard to justify and it looks to candidates as if it has been done subjectively.* [25]

Other advice given to returning officers includes a stress on the need to deal with candidates fairly. There is also a discussion of direct and indirect discrimination. Referring to the latter, the literature states: 'you are not able to use whether or not they have a husband or a wife, supportive or not, or several children or not, as factors in the process'. There is also an appreciation that fairness does not necessarily mean sameness: in a section looking at the relationship between the returning officer and candidates, the guidance is that 'a softer line may be more appropriate for a "fragile flower" type of candidate'. At the hustings meetings candidates cannot be asked about financial contributions nor can questions be asked 'which discriminate against groups such as women or candidates with disabilities'. The Party's literature also states that whilst 'it is not illegal to discriminate on the grounds of, say, age or sexual orientation' this is 'very unwise' and 'not in the spirit of the Party'.

The 2005 General Election: evaluating party strategies to increase the numbers of women MPs

The result of the general election saw 128 women MPs elected to the House of Commons – an increase of 10 from 2001. Yet, despite Labour losing seats in 2005, there has been no significant inter-party re-balancing: Labour remains the party with the highest number (98) and percentage (27.5) of women MPs. In percentage terms women Liberal Democrat MPs constitute 16.1 per cent of all their MPs while Conservative women constitute only 8.6 per cent. The comparative figures for 2001 were 23.7 per cent, 9.6 per cent and 8.6 per cent (Labour, Liberal Democrat, and Conservative) respectively. So, while it is true that the Conservative Party made gains in the number of its women MPs (from 14 in 2001 to 17 in 2005), they are flatlining in percentage terms; despite doubling their representation this time, the Liberal Democrats remain on much smaller numbers.

The explanation for the relative success of each party's women candidates lies in the type of seats for which they were selected. Table 6 below shows the distribution of women candidates by type of seat.

TABLE 6: WOMEN CANDIDATES BY TYPE OF SEAT 2005				
	Seats won in 2001	Winnable 5%	Winnable 10%	Unwinnable	Total
Labour	115	2	2	47	166
Con	14	4	7	93	118
LibDem	4	2	5	114	125

Note: the type of seat calculated using the 2001 election results. Seats are deemed winnable if the party won the seat in 2001 or came second within a margin of less than five per cent or less than 10 per cent, all other seats are classified as unwinnable.

Women Labour candidates, were, then, most likely to be selected in seats the Party was defending, rather than those it had failed to win in 2001 and was unlikely to gain in 2005. This was due directly to the implementation of AWS in 30 of Labour's vacant held seats. In contrast, the majority of women Conservative candidates were placed not in the seats it held, but in those where it had been placed third last time or where the majority achieved by the winning party in 2001 had been greater than 10 per cent. Consequently, it did not matter that the party selected 50 per cent women candidates in either its CSI or primary seats - the Conservative's innovative selection mechanisms were themselves located in the Party's unwinnable constituencies. Turning to the Liberal Democrats, they also selected more women in constituencies that were unwinnable and fewer in their own vacant seats, although the Party did make a number of gains in places defined as unwinnable - not least in Solihull and Hornsey and Wood Green.

TABLE 7: WOMEN MPS ELECTED IN 2005 BY TYPE OF SEAT				
	Seats won in 2001	Winnable 5%	Winnable 10%	Unwinnable	Total
Labour	98	0	0	0	98
Con	14	1	1	1	17
LibDem	4	1	1	4	10

Thus, in contrast to both the Conservative and Liberal Democrat parties, and despite the fact that it experienced a net lost of 47 seats at the 2005 general election, Labour, by using AWS to select women in the seats where the sitting MP stood down, managed to increase both the number and percentage of its women MPs. All Labour's new women MPs were returned from seats the Party held in 2001. It may not have topped its 1997 high-water mark of 101 women MPs, but it did at least reverse its 2001 decline – no mean feat in an election where it lost nine sitting women MPs. These losses were largely compensated by the election of 23 of the 30 women elected in AWS seats.

Comparing Labour's successes in getting women elected at the last three elections (in 1997 the Party jumped from 37 to 101 Labour women MPs; in 2001 it returned only 95) a clear relationship with the use of equality guarantees is evident: the numbers of women MPs increase when Labour uses equality guarantees (in 1997 and 2005) and declines when it does not (in 2001) (see Table 1). While it is clear that the use of AWS by the Labour Party delivered, this is not to say that the policy did not generate a backlash. Indeed, the high profile defeat of a Labour woman at the 2005 election in Blanaeu Gwent, at the hands of ex-Labour Assembly Member, Peter Law was hailed as an anti-AWS victory. However, this loss is likely to also reflect wider anti-New Labour feelings, as well as a perception that an outsider had been imposed.

The loss of Blaenau Gwent notwithstanding, Labour's use of AWS should be secure for the foreseeable future. In the past, when the policy has been criticised, many of Labour's women MPs have publicly defended AWS and there is no reason to suspect that they would act differently now. In the future, the Party needs to consider the use of AWS for Scottish seats (exempt for the 2005 election because of the reduction in Scottish seats) and whether it is willing to advocate hybrid

BME and All Women Shortlists. With the defeat of Oona King, Labour is left again with only two Black women MPs: Dawn Butler and Diane Abbott. The failure of any BME women candidates to be selected on AWS at the 2005 general election reflects in part Labour's informal decision to locate them predominantly in constituencies without significant BME populations, and might indicate a lack of local supply. But, the case of Dawn Butler who was unsuccessful in West Ham on an AWS but successful in the open, but, by default, all black shortlist for Brent South, suggests there may well be a question of Party demand to be addressed.

In contrast to Labour's successes in 2005, the Conservative Party continues to have a problem in converting women candidates into women MPs, despite significant efforts to reform their approval processes and the introduction of innovative selection procedures. In simple terms this is because local associations did not select women candidates in sufficient numbers in Conservative held or winnable seats. The failure to improve the *percentage* of women MPs in the parliamentary party between 2001 and 2005 suggests the Conservatives should reconsider their position *vis a vis* equality guarantees – something that some of the contenders in the Party leadership election have begun to do but, at the time of writing, have not taken a strong position on. In September 2005, Theresa May advocated a 100-strong 'A' list of approved candidates made up of 50 women and 50 men to be selected for the Party's top 100 winnable seats. Such a list could have a substantial impact, as long as women are equally distributed throughout the list. [26]

The return of 10 women Liberal Democrat MPs, representing a 100 per cent increase on their 2001 numbers looks, at least on first view, to suggest that equality guarantees are not a necessary condition of women's greater political representation. It might be that a cultural transformation has occurred within the Liberal Democrats so that women no longer face selectorate discrimination; or perhaps the Party's one-third sex quota at the shortlisting stage was sufficient to force local parties to consider greater numbers of women candidates, who then decided that the woman was, after all, the best candidate. However, it will not be until the next election that it becomes clear whether this year's successes were achieved more by luck than design – many of the Liberal Democrat's new women MPs were not selected in its most winnable seats but appeared to benefit from unexpected swings in the Party's favour.

Women's Political Representation: comparing Westminster, the Scottish Parliament, the National Assembly for Wales and the Northern Ireland Assembly

Comparing the levels of women's political representation within a single state enables analysis that is, in effect, comparing 'like cases': it is less likely that there are significant socio-economic and cultural differences within the UK that can account for large differences in the respective levels of women's representation. If anything, the Celtic fringes of the UK have had poorer levels of women's representation in the past than Westminster, and in the Welsh case a reputation for being less than amenable to women in politics (Edwards and McAllister 2002). Yet, with women's 50 per cent presence in the National Assembly for Wales and the 40 per cent in the Scottish Parliament following the 2003 elections, the devolved institutions compare favourably with the 20 per cent of women MPs in Parliament (as Table 3 above showed). Returning to Norris and Lovenduski's explanatory framework, the situation in Scotland, Wales and Northern Ireland differs from Westminster at the *systemic* level - with different electoral and party systems; in terms of the parties' organisation, rules and ideology - not least because of the existence of nationalist parties and transformed inter-party competition; and with respect to electoral outcomes, with multi-party government and legislative presence. Moreover, the establishment of the devolved institutions under Labour's constitutional reform programme provided a new opportunity to achieve women's greater political representation (Dobrowolsky and Hart 2003).

Reflecting on the possible explanations for the differing levels of women's representation in the different national political institutions within the UK, the most obvious candidate is the use of proportional representation. Cross-national studies consistently demonstrate that proportional representation is more favourable to the election of women (Norris 2004). Indeed, the most common assumption made about the relatively high percentage of women elected to these new institutions in 1999 was that the electoral system used had been influential. However, close analysis suggests that this was in fact not the case. In Scotland and Wales the experience of a mixed electoral system, involving both PR and majoritarian aspects, is one example of where PR was neither a necessary nor sufficient condition: the gains for women's representation were made not in the PR seats but in the FPTP seats, as Tables 8 and 9 demonstrate:

TABLE 8: MAJOR PARTY WOMEN MSPS ELECTED IN 1999 AND 2003								
	Labour		Liberal Democrat		Conservative		SNP	
	1999	2003	1999	2003	1999	2003	1999	2003
Regions	2	2	2	1	3	4	13	7
Constituency	26	26	0	1	0	0	2	2

Amended from B. Gill, *Winning Women: Lessons from Scotland and Wales* (London: Fawcett Society), p. 8 and CAWP.

TABLE 9: MAJOR PARTY WOMEN AMS ELECTED THROUGH REGIONS/ CONSTITUENCIES 1999 AND 2003								
	Labour		Liberal Democrat		Conservative		PC	
	1999	2003	1999	2003	1999	2003	1999	2003
Regions	0	0	2	1	3	2	4	5
Constituency	15	19	1	2	0	0	2	1

Amended from B. Gill, *Winning Women: Lessons from Scotland and Wales* (London: Fawcett Society), p. 8 and CAWP.

With the explanation for the success in women's representation lying with the constituency seats, attention shifts away from a simplistic reasoning about the impact of a particular electoral system to the nature of party competition and, in Scotland and Wales, parties' evaluation about their likely success in either the constituency or the regional seats. Moreover, and fully in line with the argument stressing the importance of political parties in creating an artificial demand for women candidates advanced in respect of Westminster, the increased levels of women's representation in the devolved institutions in 1999 and 2003 reflect the use of equality guarantees, especially by Labour, the most successful party electorally in both countries. This is not to say that the nationalist parties and inter-party dynamics played no role (Chaney 2004, 291). There was also inter-country dynamics at play – decisions made by the parties in Scotland prior to 1999 affected decisions in Wales (Russell et al 2002, 73).

The higher levels of women's representation secured in Scotland and Wales - often referred to as a gender coup - did not just happen as a natural consequence of devolution (Mackay et al 2003), but reflected the use of equality guarantees by particular parties. These measures themselves reflected women's activism to engender the devolved institutions. In the words of Mackay and her colleagues, women 'took advantage of the institutional, political and discursive opportunities that the devolution debate...presented' (ibid, 85). In Scotland this brought together a wide coalition of women's organisations over a period of 10 years who argued that 'new politics' could not be new if Scotland's institutions merely reproduced male domination. Women's representation became, in effect, entwined with devolution. However, since devolution, the principle of parity of representation between women and men, and the associated commitment to equality guarantees, has become more entrenched in Wales than in Scotland (Mackay 2004, 156). In Scotland, gender parity has slipped down the political agenda whereas, in Wales, with Labour and PC employing equality guarantees, a dynamic has been created which influenced the behaviour of the other parties. Thus, by the time of the 2003 elections, the more systematic strategies used in Wales to increase women's representation outflanked the Scots' reliance on 'luck' rather than design (Mackay 2003).

Labour

The Labour Party's decision to 'twin' constituency seats in both Scotland and Wales in 1999 reflected the reality that it was most likely to win constituency rather than regional seats. Constituencies were 'twinned' on the basis of 'winnability' and proximity, and a male and female candidate selected for each pair of seats. The strategy was widely supported by grassroots women in Scotland and Labour women MPs, although the Party leadership also recognised electoral reasons to support the policy. It would, *inter alia*, signal the Party's 'modern' identity and distinguish the new institutions from (tarnished) Labour local government; it would help see off electoral competition from the SNP; and would preempt the establishment of a women's party, something that seemed a possibility. In Wales, despite greater intra-party hostility, including the Welsh party leadership's extreme hostility to any form of equality guarantees, twinning was agreed, albeit on a 51.95 per cent vote in 1998 (Russell, et al 2002, 57-9).

43

Perhaps surprisingly, given Labour's lead on equality guarantees in Scotland, the Party in 2003 chose not to twin – the policy had only been intended for single use. Instead, it relied on incumbency in its constituency seats to return women MSPs, although women were placed in first position in two regions where it stood the greatest chance of being successful (Mackay 2004, 151-2). In contrast, Welsh Labour were the first party to take advantage of the Sex Discrimination (EC) Act and used AWS in six constituency seats, although not without significant local hostility, once again. [27]

SNP

Supportive of the principle of a sex-balanced Scottish Parliament in the run up to the first election, and with its successes likely to come in the regional lists, it was expected that the SNP would 'zip' its regional lists. But, despite support from women activists, such a policy was rejected. Fortunately, exhortation by the leadership combined with electoral competition with Labour - the so-called contagion effect - alongside pressure from women party activists, resulted in women being selected near the top of their regional lists. In 2003, however, the SNP again chose not to use equality guarantees and failed to place women in favourable positions on the regional lists. [28]

Plaid Cymru

Facing electoral competition in 1999 from a Labour Party committed to twinning – and therefore likely to see the election of significant numbers of women AMs – Plaid Cymru was encouraged to address the issue of equality guarantees even though they were concerned about the prospect of intra-party conflict (Russell et al 2002, 61). Under pressure from senior women, and looking to win votes from Labour, the party leadership was persuaded to implement a 'gender template' in the regional seats, where it was expected to be electorally successful:

women were guaranteed first and third place on each of the five regional lists. In 2003, the Party acted again and placed women in the first two places on each regional list.

The Liberal Democrats and the Conservative Party

Neither the Liberal Democrats nor the Conservative Party used equality guarantees in the 1999 and 2003 elections to the Scottish Parliament and National Assembly for Wales. The Liberal Democrats used sex 'balanced shortlists' in Scotland in 1999 but took no action in Wales in 1999; in 2003 its efforts in Wales, although less so in Scotland, were focused on enforcing this rule and exhorting candidates to come forward if there was a shortage of candidates of either sex (Mackay 2004, 152). Meanwhile the Conservative Party made 'no serious moves to adopt' equality guarantees for any of the elections (Russell 2002, 65).

Northern Ireland

The sectarian political division in Northern Ireland has historically limited women's political representation. However, and in contrast to the opportunities provided by the new constitutional settlements in Scotland and Wales, the low proportion of women representatives in the Northern Irish Assembly - 14 per cent in 1998 and 17 per cent in 2003 - is reflective of the general trend in women's numerical representation where quotas are not in operation. The formation of the Northern Ireland Women's coalition (NIWC) put forward women candidates to stand for election and brought media attention to the male dominance of politics in Northern Ireland (Ward 1997). But ultimately they had little impact upon the selection of more women candidates by the other parties (Ward 2004). Despite manifesto commitments to equality of opportunity made by all of the parties prior to the 2003 election, sex balanced shortlists of candidates were not realised.

Section 1 Conclusion:
Women's Representation in UK Politics

The relative successes of the women candidates for the Conservative, Liberal Democrat and Labour Parties at the 2005 general election illustrates that whilst a small increase in the number of women MPs can be achieved without the use of equality guarantees, such as occurred in the Liberal Democrat Party in 2005, larger numbers seem to require the use of equality guarantees, not least to ensure that women are selected in substantial numbers in winnable and party held seats. All three political parties could have made use of the new opportunities provided by the Sex Discrimination (Election Candidates) Act in 2005. But, with only Labour using equality guarantees, it was always going to be hard for there to be a significant improvement in the numbers of women elected especially when the one party using them was likely to see a swing against it at the election. Any losses on Labour's side would need to have been filled by the Conservatives and the Liberal Democrats. A future election that sees a reduction in Labour MPs – and women sit in 12 of the 43 new hyper-marginal Labour seats – at the expense of parties that do not use equality guarantees is more than likely going to witness a substantial decline in the numbers of women MPs.

Comparing the situation at Westminster with the devolved institutions further illustrates the importance of equality guarantees. Constitutional reform provided a unique opportunity to create new political institutions, elected by proportional representation, and around which women mobilised to ensure the greater representation of women in politics. Nonetheless, the success in returning comparatively large numbers of women in both Scotland and Wales reflects the decision by some political parties to employ equality guarantees.

[6] Following the death of Patsy Calton, Liberal Democrat MP for Cheadle, just after the election, the number of women MPs is, as of October 2005, 127.

[7] This table is comprised of data from the 2000 Hansard Society report *Women at the Top: Cracking the Glass Ceiling* and data collected by the Hansard Society following the 2001 and 2005 general elections.

[8] This figure includes Sylvia Heal, First Deputy Chairman of Ways and Means.

[9] Updated 2003 by-election.

[10] This figure includes the late Patsy Calton, see footnote 1 above.

[11] This figure does not include the constituency of South Staffordshire where the election was suspended due to the death of the Liberal Democrat candidate.

[12] As the later discussion of Equal Opportunities practices in, and reforms of, the parties' selection procedures indicate, the parties have acted to minimise the likelihood of overt discrimination.

[13] The placement of women candidates is discussed later in the Report. In brief, as Tables 3 and 4 show in the absence of equality guarantees that create and impose an artificial demand on party selectorates, party selectorates seem to prefer to select men.

[14] This refers to the practice whereby, in designated AWS seats, the constituency party shortlist and select their parliamentary candidate from a list of aspirant candidates all of whom must be women.

[15] The passage of this legislation and the role of women therein, are discussed in greater detail in Section 2 of this Report.

[16] The Act's permissive nature also negated likely opposition from those who oppose positive discrimination *per se* (Childs 2002).

[17] The Party also had a Black and Minority Ethnic (BME) quota at the shortlisting stage: 'Should one or more black or Asian members of the national panel express an interest in selection, the Executive [of the CLP] will have to meet by the close of nominations to make a nomination from those interested'. (*Labour's Future*, 7).

[18] Scotland, was excluded from this process because of the impact of the reduction of Scottish Parliamentary seats at the 2005 general election.

[19] It is also allowed for some questions and responses to be in languages other than English (*Labour's Future*, 77).

[20] In AWS the second sentence is removed from the declaration.

[21] Each list exists only for each Parliament and there is no automatic renewal. Individuals have two chances to be approved, although under exceptional circumstances further chances may be offered. Only MPs who take the Conservative whip are on the parliamentary list, which accounts for Howard Flight's problem at the 2005 general election.

[22] Intellectual skills were also part of the PAB assessment.

[23] There was a requirement that those seeking to register were on the electoral register for the particular constituency.

[24] In 2002, the Liberal Democratic Party conference voted to row back on its previously successful experiment with 'zipping' in European elections (Lovenduski 2005).

[25] If there are fewer than three candidates and/or if there are too few women or men, then the returning officer consults with the regional candidates' chair as to whether the selection proceeds. In certain cases a shortlist of one is acceptable – the rules do not identify but imply that this most likely in unwinnable seats.

[26] Speech to the Fawcett Society September 2005.

[27] A BME woman was selected, but ultimately unsuccessful, in one of the five list places reserved for BME candidates (Mackay 2004).

[28] The small Scottish Socialist Party sex balanced its lists.

SECTION 2
Making a Difference and Acting for Women?

Section 2 of the Report opens with a brief summary of the arguments that are made in support of the case for women's political presence. It then considers in greater depth the specific argument that women's descriptive and substantive representation are linked. In so doing it adopts a judicious take on the concept of critical mass – the widely accepted framework that is used to hypothesise when women in politics are able to effect change. In contrast, we argue that the determinants of the substantive representation of women are more complicated than a simple function of their number.

Through the use of case studies from Westminster, the Scottish Parliament and National Assembly for Wales, examples are provided of occasions in each case where the substantive representation of women has occurred. [29] Whether women politicians have a different political style and can change the norms and working practices of their institutions is also discussed and the way in which gender framed the debates about the reform of Parliament's hours is included to show how gender can be cross cut by other identities and interests. Qualified by an acknowledgement that it is probably impossible to prove a direct causal relationship between women's presence in politics (descriptive representation) and their substantive representation or to quantify the difference women make, the analysis suggests, nonetheless, that women do make a difference and 'act for' women.

Introduction

> **House of Commons Case Study:**
>
> **The Gendering of Parliamentary Questions**
>
> Analysis of oral and written questions in the 1997-1998 Parliamentary session reveals sex differences in the use of the terms 'women', 'men' and 'gender' by MPs: nearly half of all women MPs but only one fifth of men MPs asked such questions; moreover, women asked 35 per cent of these questions, greater than their overall proportion in Parliament (18 per cent); a higher proportion of women MPs than men MPs also asked a question that included the term 'women'; and women were no less likely to use written rather than oral questions, whereas the men preferred written questions. Comparing parties, women Labour MPs are proportionately less likely to ask questions than women in the other parties – a finding that is related to the small number of Conservative and Liberal Democrat women, who are presumably compensating for the lack of female colleagues by speaking more often. Sixteen substantive issues are identified in the questions containing the term 'woman', with the top four being women's employment, domestic violence, politics and representation and women's health. Nonetheless, this research does not suggest a dramatic feminisation of the parliamentary agenda: 27 per cent of MPs and only one per cent of all parliamentary questions in the session included any of the terms women, men and gender (Bird 2005).

It was Labour's first landslide election in 1997 that transformed the face of British politics. Although constituting less than 20 per cent of the House of Commons, a record 120 women were returned as MPs, 101 of them Labour, of whom 65 were newly elected. As the now infamous photograph of Tony Blair surrounded by Labour's women MPs symbolised, the 1997 general election witnessed the insertion of women into the UK Parliament and government - the first meaning of feminisation; it would take time to see whether it would give rise to the integration of women's perspectives and concerns, the term's second meaning (Lovenduski 2005, 12). Expectations of the latter were, nonetheless, high. The general public found it reasonable, and the women MPs were confident that, as they entered Parliament, they would bring with them their experiences, views and concerns (Childs 2004).

Fast forward to 2005. There are two different readings of whether women's concerns and perspectives have been integrated into politics: in the first, seen through the prism of the 2005 general election campaign, UK parliamentary politics remains as male dominated and masculinised as before (Childs 2005; Campbell and Lovenduski 2005): the key election issues were those of trust, asylum and immigration, Iraq and the economy – 'women's issues' were rarely mentioned; the campaign itself was a three-way fight between the male party leaders interpreted by 'alpha male' political commentators in testosterone-fuelled encounters - women ministers, MPs, and commentators were largely 'off stage'.

In the second account, feminisation is apparent: the number of women MPs increased slightly at the election, and there is a record six Cabinet Members.[30] Patricia Hewitt's promotion to Health Secretary is the only visible gain for women in the Cabinet, with the remainder reappointed to their previous positions or to similar posts. Thus Hilary Armstrong continues as Chief Whip, Margaret Becket leads the Department of the Environment, Valerie Amos, once the Executive Director of the Equal Opportunities Commission leads the House of Lords, while Tessa Jowell adds the women's portfolio to Culture, Media and Sport. Twenty-six women MPs and Peers were appointed to other positions in government and most Departments of State have women ministers, although the Cabinet Office, the Ministry of Defence, the Foreign and Commonwealth Office, the Department for International Development, the Northern Ireland Office, and the Law Officer's Department are male bastions. In a return to form, the Minister for Women (Parliamentary Under-Secretary), Meg Munn is not to be paid, just like her predecessor in 1997 Joan Ruddock (*Guardian* 16 May 2005; Childs 2004, 166).

'Women's concerns', including the work/life balance, maternity/paternity leave and pay and childcare, have also moved towards the centre of political debate and constitute issues over which parties now compete, not least for women's votes (*Guardian* 4 March 2005). As Polly Toynbee argues, the Conservative Party's manifesto commitment to childcare was, yet 'one more symbol of how far Labour has shunted the ideological tectonic plates' (*Guardian* 30 March 2005; Childs 2005). Furthermore, and despite the apparent failure of the mainstream media to address these issues, the three main parties, along with a number of women journalists, went to great efforts to ensure that they were addressed in the mainstream and 'women's media' – for example, on the BBC's *Woman's Hour* and in women's magazines such as *Vogue, Cosmopolitan and Glamour*.

To what extent is this feminisation of UK politics a reflection of the greater numbers of women in Parliament? The first point to make is that feminisation is a process rather than an end point – so talk of the feminisation of politics is about the relative integration of women's concerns and perspectives into political discourse and policy. The second point is that proving direct causal relationships between the presence of women and broad feminised change is probably impossible, as later discussions in this section will contend. However, and despite this qualification, circumstantial evidence is highly suggestive: looking back at the 1997-2005 Labour governments, policies on childcare, Sure Start, the extension of maternity and paternity rights, rights to flexible working, equal pay and domestic violence have been championed by senior Labour women ministers, including amongst others Tessa Jowell, Patricia Hewitt, Margaret Hodge and Harriet Harman (Toynbee and Walker 2005).

Importantly, claims that women politicians put women's concerns and perspectives onto the political table do not imply that women's concerns have never hitherto been addressed in political institutions dominated by men or that some of these issues would not have come onto the political agenda in the absence of women. But what they do contend is that the sex of our representatives matters. A weak interpretation of this suggests that women representatives, by introducing new perspectives or approaches, will 'make a difference'. The stronger claim is that women are more likely to substantively represent (act for) women.

House of Commons Case Study:
Sex Differences in the Signing of Early Day Motions

Early Day Motions (EDMs) – parliamentary motions for which there is no debate – have long been studied as indicators of MPs' attitudes, beliefs, and priorities (Berrington 1973). Analysis of the signing of EDMs in the 1997 Parliament by Labour backbench MPs shows that Labour's women were disproportionately signing 'women's' EDMs and especially those motions that were also coded feminist (Childs and Withey 2004). Crucially, these sex differences are evident despite women's lesser propensity to sign EDMs in general. Establishing sex differences in the signing of EDMs is important: they constitute a clear example of behavioural differences between women and men MPs with women acting for women and doing so in a feminist direction.

They are also suggestive of how Labour's women MPs might act if other parliamentary activities were as relatively unconstrained as EDMs. Taking little effort and with few costs, EDMs constitute a 'safe' parliamentary activity in which women MPs should feel free to sign those they support. Nonetheless, a key limitation of this analysis is that whilst it constitutes evidence of behavioural sex differences and demonstrates a feminisation of the political agenda, it cannot tell us whether the women MPs' actions had an effect in terms of the feminisation of legislation.

The case for women's political presence: the substantive representation of women

As previous Hansard Society Reports have noted, the case for women's political presence can be made on a number of different grounds: for reasons of justice; symbolic representation; because women's interests are discounted in the absence of women's political presence; and because women will introduce a different set of values and concerns (Phillips 1995). Not all these arguments link women's presence to women making a difference or substantively representing (acting for) women.

Justice arguments carry no such expectations, contending only that women's under-representation is evidence of a *prima facie* case of injustice that should be redressed (Phillips 1995, 65). Arguments based on symbolic representation do not necessarily link descriptive and substantive representation either. It is rather that overwhelmingly male political institutions 'look wrong', seem to suggest that women are not capable of being representatives and undermine legitimacy in our political institutions. For such reasons, women's physical presence is necessary to demonstrate women's equality and to alter the perception of politics as a male domain (Sapiro 1998, 183). However, women's symbolic presence can offer the possibility of substantive effects through a role model effect: not only might women think of themselves as able, and encourage women to participate in politics when they see women 'doing' politics, others might actually gain political experience by working for women representatives (Clark 1994, 100).

Derived from the distinction drawn by Hanna Pitkin, in her seminal work *The Concept of Representation*, 'acting for' representation refers to a relationship in which the representative is 'responsive' to the represented (Pitkin 1967, 140). Those who claim a relationship between women's descriptive and substantive representation contend that women representatives will, on the basis of their gendered experiences, 'act for' women.[31] This claim implies that women's concerns *and* women's perspectives on all issues will be articulated (Lovenduski 1997). 'Women's concerns' refers to those issues in which the primary subject matter are 'particularly salient to', or 'have a more immediate and direct impact on' women (Reingold 2000), whether for 'biological or social' reasons (Lovenduski 1997, 708).

Accordingly, abortion, childcare, constitutional equality guarantees, divorce, domestic violence, equal pay, family issues, parental leave, pensions, rape, reproductive rights, women as carers, women's health, the work/life balance, and issues historically regarded as in the private sphere, are widely identified as 'women's concerns'.[32]

Voting Behaviour Case Study:
Women in the Electorate

Analysis of the 2001 UK general election found that women were more likely than men to state that health and education were their most important election issues. Men, on the other hand, were more likely to prioritise the economy and taxation. There were further differences within age groups. Older women tended to be more right-leaning, but younger women were more left-leaning in their political attitudes than younger men and were also more likely to hold feminist values. Focus group research conducted prior to the 2005 general election found similar differences in women and men's issue priorities (Campbell 2006).

There is a danger here, though, of eliding the *substantive* representation of women with feminist substantive representation – presuming that women representatives will act for women in a feminist way. Hence, a distinction between feminist, anti-feminist and neutral definitions of women's concerns and perspectives needs to be drawn. Importantly, what constitutes women's concerns and feminist, anti-feminist or neutral positions on these vary over time and space, and can be contested even amongst women. So while feminists in the West might agree that feminist legislation is that which sets out to 'achieve role equity (the extension of rights to women) or role change for women' (transformation of women's dependent role) (Swers 2002) while anti-feminist legislation inhibits role change and restricts access to abortion (Reingold 2000, 166), non-feminists, and feminists elsewhere, may disagree.

Making the claim that women should be present in politics for substantive reasons, whilst an important mobilising force for women's political participation (Mackay 2001), is the most contested argument for women's political presence. It can set up an unhealthy expectation that women representatives are in a position to transform the content of politics by bringing women's concerns and perspectives to the political table.

National Assembly for Wales Case Study: Analysis of Plenary Debates [33]

Analysis of more than three million words of text from the plenary debates of the National Assembly for Wales during its first term (1999-2003) finds evidence of sex differences: women AMs were significantly more likely than their male colleagues to engage in debate on women's concerns (domestic violence, childcare, equal pay for work of equal value) (Chaney forthcoming). Women constituted approximately two-thirds to three-quarters of all such interventions. Women were also significantly more likely than men to initiate debate on gender equality issues. Moreover, in the discussion of women's concerns, women were significantly more likely than men to make pro-feminist interventions – 86 per cent compared to 14 per cent, respectively. Finally, women predominate in the ministerial interjections, again accounting for two-thirds to three-quarters of all such interventions. Greater proportions of women AMs participated in the articulation of women's concerns than men AMs: 67 per cent compared to 36 per cent, respectively; half of all women AMs participated in debates on domestic violence and equal pay, while three-quarters participated in debates on childcare and other issues. The research also identifies 'critical actors', women who disproportionately articulate women's concerns – between one third and one half of all women's interventions in these debates.

The Concept of Critical Mass

The conceptual framework that is usually employed to hypothesise the relationship between women's descriptive and substantive representation is 'critical mass'. Taken from nuclear physics it refers to the quantity needed to start a chain reaction. As applied to politics, it is taken to mean that 'political behaviour, institutions, and public policy' will be transformed once women reach 'critical mass' (Studlar and McAllister 2002). The application of critical mass to the study of gender and politics derives from Rosabeth Moss Kanter's classic analysis of women's token status in a US corporation in the 1970s (Kanter 1977a, 1977b). Kanter's basic proposition is that as the numerical proportions within a group 'begin to shift so do social experiences' (Kanter 1977b, 207). Just like her token women in the American corporation, token women politicians are too few in number to influence the culture of the dominant group (Kanter 1977a, 1977b).

Critical mass theory holds out the promise of a time when women are able to substantively represent women and feminise politics: if in skewed groups (a ratio of 85:15), the numerically many – dominants – 'control the group and its culture' when women's political representation becomes tilted (ratio of 65:35) they will be able to effect change (Kanter 1977a, 966). [34] This is, for those with a commitment to women's substantive representation, an attractive claim: on the one hand, critical mass can be used to explain away the failure of women thus far – on the basis that most political institutions do not have a critical mass of women; and on the other hand, it points to a future when women will be able to make a difference and act for women just as soon as they constitute a higher percentage of legislators. As mentioned earlier, the widely accepted percentage for critical mass, held by many activists, including the UN, is 30 per cent (Dahlerup 1988).

Critical mass theory relies on two assumptions: first, that women representatives want to act for women and secondly, that the percentage of women present in a political institution is the key determinant of their behaviour and effects. Furthermore, these claims are themselves premised upon additional, unsubstantiated assumptions: first, that representatives' attitudes directly and straightforwardly translate into behaviour; secondly, that their actions will have a transformative effect. Both of these claims belie the context in which women act: evidence to date suggests that these can be to a lesser or greater extent favourable to the articulation of women's concerns and perspectives.

By returning to Kanter's original exposition, it is possible to get a better understanding of the likely impact of women's descriptive representation. Kanter makes three claims as she reflects on how minority/majority dynamics might change in the transition from a skewed to a tilted group (Childs and Krook 2005). The first two point in different directions, whilst the third adds a new dimension to our understanding, by focusing on the role of feminist women:

1 With an increase in relative numbers, minority members are potentially allies, can form coalitions, and can affect the culture of the group

2 With an increase in relative numbers, minority members begin to become individuals differentiated from each other (Kanter 1977a, 966)

3 Even when numbers remain low, if tokens are highly identified with their own group (feminist or 'women identified women') then the problems of tokenism can be overcome (Kanter, 1977a, 987, 1977b 238)

Recognising that Kanter makes not a single claim but three is an important corrective to the widely accepted theory of critical mass. Not only does she signal the possibility that greater numbers of women in politics can lead to an increased diversity of women with different identities, attitudes and behaviours – implying that we should not make confident claims about the inevitability of critical mass delivering women's substantive representation or feminisation – her third claim suggests that the proportions of women present in a particular political forum may matter less than the presence of feminist/women-identified- women.

Appreciating the totality of Kanter's ideas throws new light on the conclusions of empirical studies that have tried to determine when women make a difference and act for women. Often this literature explains the failure of women to effect policy change by identifying the opportunities and constraints they face.[35] These include, *inter alia*:

- Institutional norms, including gendered institutional norms

- Political party affiliation, referring both to ideological division and party cohesion and loyalty

- Roles and positions within an institution, for example, legislative experience or membership of institutional committees

- The presence or absence of gender machinery, including informal women's committees or a more formal women's caucus

- The external political environment, including the electoral system and the presence or absence of healthy women's/feminist civil society

It is reasonable to assume that where women and men face the 'same institutional norms and expectations and share the same status', they are more likely than not going to act in similar ways (Reingold 2000, 116), although as gendered institutions, political institutions are additionally likely to constrain women as indirect discrimination and sexism act to police their behaviour (Yoder 1991; Puwar 2004). At the same time, political institutions are not single spaces, so women's experiences of constraints and opportunities are likely to vary within them. Moreover, women representatives do not have a single role or position within that institution. They may be new or long-established; be members of the government or opposition; backbenchers or part of the institution's structures.

Women representatives are also likely to be a diverse group, and identities other than gender are likely to influence their attitudes and behaviour. Women's race, age, and class identities (at the very least) are likely to intersect with their gender identities. In party democracies, party identity is likely to be a particularly strong influence and, where predominant, such as in the UK House of Commons, liable to reduce the space for women representatives to act other than in line with their party, even if it does not always function as a constraint to the same degree across all parliamentary activity.

Trying to test the critical mass hypothesis by controlling for all the possible mediating factors is arguably a pointless and probably impossible empirical task – there are so few political institutions that meet Kanter's strict criteria of a tilted group. The nature of the relationship between the proportion of women present in politics and their effects is better captured by shifting from examining *when* women make a difference (that is, trying to establish what proportion of women is necessary) to exploring *how* the substantive representation of women occurs in particular political places (Childs and Krook 2005). In practice, this suggests that researchers should engage in detailed analyses that trace the behaviour of representatives over time in order to uncover the respective roles of women as 'critical actors' in the substantive representation of women.

Research should, then, examine whether the critical actors are ordinary members of the Parliament or whether they are members of the government or institutional hierarchy. Although many studies investigate the impact of women without drawing this distinction, it is possible that being a member of the government or having a position of power within an institution (for example, as chair of a parliamentary committee) provides greater opportunities to substantively represent women. The functional division of labour between women and men in government, where women are more likely to have responsibility for 'soft' policy areas might mean that women are provided with greater opportunities to act for women in respect of health, cultural affairs, education and social welfare. [36]

Research should also look beyond the individual or collective actions of women. Treating women representatives as discrete individuals seeking to act for women in isolation may also misrepresent the networks within which women representatives, just like any other representatives, act. Research therefore needs to consider the role of women representatives alongside other possible actors including, but not limited to, gender machinery, (such as the UK Women and Equality Unit), women's groups in civil society, wider 'feminist advocacy coalitions' and non-feminist allies in government (Mazur 2002, 191-5). [37]

House of Commons Case Study:
The Reduction of VAT on Sanitary Products

A reduction in VAT from 17.5 per cent to five per cent on sanitary products was announced at the 2000 Budget. In so doing, the Chancellor Gordon Brown was reacting to a campaign by the backbench Labour woman MP Christine McCafferty. While it is the case that the Treasury had considered the issue just after the 1997 general election, and that the Minister responsible Dawn Primarolo was in favour in principle, McCafferty should be considered a critical actor in this policy change. Her three-year campaign in Parliament, with the tabling of three EDMs, was widely supported by MPs: they received, in total, more than 250 signatures and in 1999/2000 her EDM was the sixth most 'signed' EDM of the parliamentary session. On two of its three outings, there were sex differences in the signing of Labour MPs, with Labour's women disproportionately signing the EDMs (Childs and Withey 2005). In addition to the pressure within Parliament, McCafferty also went public: the immediate trigger for the Treasury's decision in 2000 was an interview that McCafferty gave on BBC Radio 4's Woman's Hour.

Scottish Parliament Case Study:
Concrete Policy Outcomes, Domestic Abuse [38]

Action against domestic abuse is widely recognised as the key achievement of the first session of the Scottish Parliament - 'the most concrete gain for a women's agenda' (Mackay 2005, 5). Substantial improvements have been made in service provision for survivors of domestic abuse; new legislation has been passed (The Protection from Abuse Act (Scotland) 2001) – the Scottish Parliament's first committee bill; and government prevention initiatives, such as media campaigns and educational work in schools, have been undertaken. The development of policy in the area of domestic abuse in Scotland constitutes a clear example of where women in civil society, (such as Scottish

Women's Aid, with more than 30 years of experience in campaigning, lobbying and service provision), parliament, and government acted for women by taking up the opportunities offered by devolution. Women have been brought into, and feminist perspectives have been institutionalised within, the policy process. These changes reflect the mobilisation, campaigning and participation of women's organisations in civil society with extensive expertise in domestic abuse, together with strong political leadership by women ministers and parliamentarians, supported by key male allies, and the secondment of a feminist domestic abuse expert into the Scottish Executive.

How do we know when women have made a difference or acted for women?

Attempts to determine whether women make a difference and/or act for women, run into problems of measurement and methods. Too often research has looked for sex differences in representatives' attitudes, behaviours, approaches and practices. This is not to say that such differences - with women, for example, being more concerned with, and acting on, women's concerns or employing a different style of politics – do not demonstrate a link between women's descriptive and substantive representation (Reingold 2000). Indeed, many of the case studies presented in this Report find sex differences and interpret this as evidence of women representatives substantively representing women. But whether *sex differences* are all that count or, to put it differently, whether the absence of sex differences necessarily proves the opposite, is a different question.

A lack of sex differences in representatives' behaviour may be caused by any number of factors: it may reflect the lack of spaces in which women can act differently and for women. A distinction between the feminisation of the political agenda (where women's concerns and perspectives are articulated) and the feminisation of legislation (where output has been transformed) should help capture occasions when women's concerns are articulated but where this has no substantive effect in terms of legislative output. It should also meet concerns that a focus on the end product of politics, such as parliamentary divisions in the House of Commons, is likely to miss the difference that women's political presence can make as they effect a re-gendering at earlier and perhaps more conducive stages of the political process (Tamerius 1995).

The absence of sex differences may also reflect diversity amongst women, with different women effectively cancelling out each other's actions. Women representatives may have a feminist consciousness, a gender consciousness (the realisation that one's sex affects one's relationship with the political world, a position that can be held by women who accept women's place is in the home and those who challenge the public/private divide) or a female consciousness (accepting of the sexual division of labour and concerned with preserving life) (Dodson 2001a).

It may also reflect a convergence in gender roles - with little difference in women and men's attitudes and behaviours – that are hidden because studies employ sex (biology) as a proxy for gender (socially constructed identities) (Swers 2002). An absence of sex differences may also be an effect of the choice of research method adopted: for example, similar behaviour at one level might hide differences at another level (in women's and men's levels of support for, or feelings towards, a particular behaviour, for example). Alternatively, the very presence of women in politics may cause men to become more concerned with women's concerns, leaving no observable or measurable sex differences in their attitudes or behaviour (Reingold 2000). Here, women are having a feminised effect over time, but not one that is necessarily visible.

Other difficulties abound with the collection and status of data: representatives' attitudes can quite easily be collected through quantitative surveys and qualitative interviews. The 2001 British Representation Study, for example, is only the latest in a series of surveys that find sex differences in respect of women's concerns (Lovenduski 2005; Lovenduski and Norris 2003) with women 'more likely to take a pro-woman line' than the men (Norris and Lovenduski 1989).[39] Such studies also find that gender gaps in respect of women's concerns go 'beyond party' (Norris 1996): on the scale measuring 'liberal' gender equality (support for equal opportunities, family and work roles and women's suitability for public office), Conservative women politicians were 'slightly more positive than male Labour politicians' (Lovenduski and Norris 2003). Such findings suggest that women MPs in all the major British political parties have a different set of values from men on issues affecting women's equality in the workplace, home and public sphere. While these attitudinal differences are not dramatic, they are consistent. They are also suggestive of political change, if and when they are translated into party manifestos, political debate and, ultimately, legislative action (Lovenduski 2005, 160).

However, attitudinal data is based on self-reported claims that – by their nature – do not permit careful examination of their actual veracity (Lovenduski and Norris 2003). Moreover the examination of women and men's attitudes is no guarantee of subsequent behaviour. In part for these reasons, a number of researchers have turned to behavioural data and statistical analysis: sceptics who do not believe women MPs' self-reported claims of acting for women can be persuaded when hard behavioural data is presented.[40] Some such data – for example, about how MPs vote – is easy to collect, particularly since the advent of electronic records posted on parliamentary websites. But this type of data can itself be limited as a test for women's substantive representation. Roll call, for example, suffers from a focus solely on the end point of legislation where women may be less free to act in accord with their attitudes, particularly in institutions characterised by party cohesion. Analysing other parliamentary behaviour, where the constraints are less determining, is often harder. There are particular difficulties gathering behavioural data in respect of activity that occurs 'behind the scenes' where representatives' actions and effects are neither observable nor measurable. While it may be possible in some instances to employ surrogate measures, these can only be suggestive.

House of Commons Case Study:
The Sex Discrimination (Election Candidates) Act 2002

Analysis of the process by which the Sex Discrimination (Election Candidates) Act 2002 was placed before Parliament reveals that there was an 'effective alliance' between women representatives, women ministers and women's groups and campaigning organisations outside Parliament acting together to get the Bill passed (Lovenduski 2001). Harriet Harman, (no longer Women's Minister but the Solicitor General) Hilary Armstrong, Patricia Hewitt (later to become Women's Minister) and Stephen Byers (Secretary of State for Transport) had to fight for its inclusion in the Queen's speech. In Parliament, the Bill had an easy passage: all the main parties welcomed the Bill, in no small way a reflection of its permissive rather then prescriptive nature. But it was women MPs and Peers – of all parties – who took a greater interest in debating the Bill's merits (Childs 2002). Men were, as has been said before, conspicuous by their absence. It might have been that they considered that the Bill, as a piece of 'women's legislation', should be debated by women, for either honourable or dishonourable reasons; alternatively, they might have been too embarrassed to speak out publicly against a Bill that was aimed at securing greater levels of women's numerical representation; or they might have thought that because the Bill was permissive rather than prescriptive that they should not waste their time on it - the real battles would come later within their parties. But, whatever their reasons, the parliamentary debates that accompanied the Sex Discrimination (Election Candidates) Act 2002 constitute another clear example of women MPs acting for women. And, on this occasion, it is possible to see the role of women in the other parties acting alongside Labour women MPs and for women: those MPs (and members of the Lords) who were more likely to favour equality guarantees and who drew on the concept of substantive representation to support the legislation were Labour members (both male and female). In contrast, those MPs who spoke against the legislation, who were hostile to positive discrimination and rejected substantive representation were mostly Conservative.

Making a difference by feminising the House of Commons?

A Women's Style of Politics Case Study:

Interviews with Labour women MPs first elected in 1997

Just under two-thirds held that women had a different style. Women prefer a 'less combative and aggressive style'. They 'don't do as much standing up, shouting on the floor of the House'. Women are more 'measured'. They prefer to adopt an approach in which one recognises 'that there will have been some merit in what was done before'. There was also a belief that the women operated not as individuals, but as part of teams: 'women will step back and ... say... "look what we have done"'. Women MPs also claimed they spoke in a different language, one that 'everybody understands' and comes from a personal perspective. At the same time some MPs recognised that younger women and men practise similar styles and that not all women practise a 'women's style of politics' – intra sex differences were accounted for on the basis of political generation and party (Childs 2004).

Turning to the impact of women's presence in the House of Commons the evidence is similarly suggestive. But there is perhaps a greater sense that Parliament has sought to and been able to resist change: women's presence and style of politics has yet to be normalised. Traditional representations of the House as an 'old boys' club', with its gladiatorial debating chamber, pink ribbon to tie up one's sword, and dark smoke-filled bars, continue to resonate and reveal the gender regime of the UK Parliament. This is manifested in rules, procedures, discourses and practices with which many men are comfortable and most women are not (Lovenduski 2005, 149).

The popular expectation following the 1997 election was that women would turn the House of Commons upside down. Similarly, in advance of the establishment of the devolved institutions, claims were made about how the more equal presence of women, combined with U-shaped debating chambers would create a 'new' political style. The new women MPs had stormed 'the most exclusive club in town' and would 'beat back pinstripe hordes'; there would be 'sweeping change for male bastion', with women overturning the 'male culture' and 'end[ing] macho politics'.[41] But before long these women were criticised for being unable to stand the heat of the parliamentary kitchen. The press repeatedly reported how they 'whinged' about the hours of the House, the 'laddish' behaviour in the Chamber, the inadequacy of the childcare provisions and because the Speaker would not allow them to breast-feed their newborn babies.[42] In the run up to the 2001 general election it was widely, albeit inaccurately, reported in the press that there was a mass exodus of Labour women MPs, first elected in 1997, too tired and tearful to return to Westminster.

Many of the women first elected in 1997 were, and still are, critical of Parliament's traditions and practices. Tess Kingham, one of only two Labour women MPs first elected in 1997 who chose not to stand for a second term, was publicly vocal, labelling male Members who engage in 'yah-boo nonsense, point-scoring and silly games' in the Chamber, 'willy-jousters' (Kingham 2001, 16). Wider criticism from the 1997 Labour intake can be seen in women's belief in, and preference for, a different 'women's' style of politics (see Case Study above).

A Women's Style of Politics Case Study:
The Scottish Parliament [43]

Women MSPs perceive that they: are at forefront of breaking down old patterns of tribal confrontational politics; developing constructive working practices in parliamentary committees; place less emphasis on oratory and the capacity to think on one's feet; prefer to engage in dialogue based on evidence and prior preparation. In contrast, male MSPs use military or games imagery to describe their practice. Finally, some male MSPs considered that the presence of a women's different style of politics allowed them to practise politics in a different way too.

The views of a wide range of British politicians, both male and female, at the local, national and sub-national level, agree that there are gendered political styles (Bochel and Briggs 2000; Norris 1996; Mackay 2005; Mackay 2004b; Makay et al 2003). However, there is a sense in which women's different approach is not considered equal to the masculinised style of male politicians. One new Labour woman MP felt that they were regarded as naïve for talking in everyday language while another recounted that one of the whips had said to her that she was 'too quiet' and that she did not do 'enough barracking and shouting'. In such a context - where the institutional framework 'demands adversarial conduct' - there is a danger that women politicians who practise a 'women's style' of politics will be judged as inferior and their impact lessened (Ross 2002). Yet, if trying to 'impose a different kind of culture is a very long-term process' (Labour woman MP), conforming to the masculinised style of politics is not necessarily straightforward either as it challenges accepted notions of femininity. As another new Labour woman MP put it: 'imagine if we all did start shouting and yelling…then we would be strident… you actually can't win'.

In addition to feelings of being 'other' and alien in the House (Childs 2004; Puwar 2004), some women MPs reveal unpleasant personal interactions with their male colleagues that include overt sexual harassment (Sones et al 2005). Anecdotal reports by Labour women MPs claim that critical comments have been made about their 'legs and breasts' and that Conservative male MPs in particular have been known 'put their hands out in front of them as if they are weighing melons' when women are speaking (Childs 2004). Such incidents, rather than suggesting that women's political presence has become normalised and accepted within politics suggest a backlash that is generated when women are perceived to be a threatening presence (Lovenduski 2005, 173). [44]

Debates about the modernisation of Parliament, in particular whether it should be reformed to be more 'family-friendly', provide a good example of the way in which representatives' gender identity is impor-tant but is also cross–cut by other identities and interests and reveals the extent to which institutions can resist change (Lovenduski 2005, 146). [45] Unlike the devolved institutions which were established from the very beginning with 'family friendly' working hours and sitting days that recognised school holidays (see Appendix 2), the House of Commons at the dawn of the new millennium largely retained a timetable largely developed to suit the needs of 19th century lawyers. They had required free mornings to perform their legal duties, before settling down to politics in the afternoon and often well into the night. Parliamentary reformers demanded that the House be brought into line with the sort of standard hours kept by most institutions. These calls met with some initial success, with a change in 2002 that meant the Commons would start earlier and sit until 7pm on Tuesdays and Wednesdays and 6pm on Thursdays. However, two years later, the House voted for a partial return to the 'good old days': following the 2005 general election sittings on Tuesday have returned to 2.30-10pm.

Analysis of a survey of MPs and candidates for the 2001 election found that overall women respondents were more likely than men to support modernisation measures that promised to have a differential impact on women (Campbell, Childs & Lovenduski 2006). For example, women were more likely to agree that MPs should work similar hours to other professions, that the working week should be shorter and that all-night sittings should be discontinued. Yet, in the debates that accompanied the reform proposals, and arguably, against expectations, intra-sex differences were also evident: established women MPs and those representing constituencies some distance from London contested many of the 1997 intake's emphasis on the importance of making the House more family-friendly and less like a gentleman's club.

The gender dimension of the reform debate went beyond the views of MPs. Those responsible for organising the 2002 vote believed that explicit reference to the gender dimensions of the reforms might cost them necessary support and tried to ensure family-friendly arguments were downplayed (Lovenduski 2005, 173). That women MPs were enjoined not to make their case in feminist terms – in order not to lose support of MPs favourable to the reforms but hostile to the new women MPs – indicates the resistance to feminised change. Nonetheless, some women MPs (for example, Caroline Flint and Oona King) continued to make the gendered case for parliamentary reform by linking it to family responsibilities even though this invited accusations of selfishly seeking to improve their own working conditions.

Section 2 Conclusion: Feminising Politics

Have the increases in the number of women present in the UK's political institutions made a difference? The summary of the literature and the individual case studies indicate that this is so. Do these examples constitute evidence that women representatives substantively represent women? Again there is evidence to suggest that it is so. Examples of where women MPs have acted for women have been detailed in the case studies presented throughout this section. In addition to the academic research highlighted here, more popular analysis is also available that reinforces the claim that there has been a feminisation of British politics over the last eight years or so (see Sones *et al* 2005).

This is not to say that it is possible to prove conclusively that there is a strong relationship between women's descriptive and substantive representation. As Lovendusksi (2005) has noted before, we cannot be absolutely sure that women representatives are making a difference, only that a difference is being made and they are part of the process. Or in the words of two Labour women MPs, one a minister: 'You can't say we have changed that but you can say we've worked six weeks on that and...change has come about' (Childs 2004); 'So is it women? I think so. Don't you think so?' (Childs and Withey 2006).

29 The Northern Ireland Assembly is not included: it has been suspended for long periods since its establishment.

30 Just two women, Caroline Spelman and Theresa May, are members of the 22 strong Shadow Cabinet.

31 Basing the substantive representation on gender and not sex avoids the twin charges of reductionism (women representatives' attitudes and behaviour are reduced back to their bodies) and essentialism (the presumption that women are a category who share a set of essential attributes).

32 More specifically related to politics, the lack of women's toilets, gyms and childcare facilities within institutions have also been identified (Geisler 2000).

33 This case study draws on the research of Paul Chaney (Cardiff University).

34 The term 'critical mass theory' is used to distinguish what is taken to be Kanter's position by much of the gender and politics literature, and what she actually claimed in her own work (Childs and Krook 2005).

35 See Childs and Krook 2005 for full details.

36 It is worth noting that whilst this functional division of labour is evident in the Cabinets of the Labour Governments, there have been some changes at the lower levels: in particular, there have been a number of women ministers, including Patricia Hewitt, Dawn Primarolo, Melanie Johnson and Ruth Kelly appointed to the Treasury, as well as Hewitt in the Department of Trade and Industry and Hazel Blears and Caroline Flint in the Home Office.

37 For a discussion of Labour's Women's Unit and Women and Equality Unit see Squires and Wickham-Jones (2002; 2004).

38 This case study draws on the research of Fiona Mackay and colleagues at the University of Edinburgh.

39 Results from the 2005 BRS will be presented by the authors of this report in 2006.

40 As one senior British political scientist told one of the authors.

41 *Independent* 13 April 1997; *Financial Times* 3 May 1997; *Telegraph* 2 May 1997; *Guardian* 3 May 1997; *Observer* 4 May 1997.

42 *Telegraph* 7 April 2001. See also *Telegraph* 22 July 2000; 8 October 2000, and *Guardian* 5 January 1998 and 3 August 2000.

43 This case study draws on the research of Fiona Mackay and colleagues at the University of Edinburgh.

44 In this though, they are arguably experiencing similar responses to other women who enter previously male-dominated occupations and where sexual harassment is similarly present.

45 The debate between reformers and traditionalists was, of course, wider than the question of Parliamentary hours. Reformers considered Parliament to be inefficient, old-fashioned, and an ineffective scrutiniser of government while the traditionalists were concerned that shorter working days and a shorting working week would make MPs look lazy, create a 'metropolitan elite' of MPs with constituencies close to Parliament, marginalise parliament, and diminish the effectiveness of parliamentary committee work.

SECTION 3
International Comparisons

Section 3 of this Report examines women's political representation, concentrating on countries that are comparable to the UK. It considers both numerical and substantive representation. All the countries share one defining feature: all are marked by the political under-representation of women, especially BME women, and the over-representation of men, especially white men. At the same time there are significant variations in the proportions of women in elected office. Such variation amongst otherwise similar countries invites comparative analysis to determine the circumstances under which women are numerically represented at higher or lower levels. In line with the analytic framework adopted in Section 1 of the Report, the importance of political institutions are highlighted as accounting for the variable levels of women's numerical representation in stable representative democracies in which the socio-economic position of women is broadly similar to that of the UK.

Introduction

The achievement of parity in women's representation globally is very much work in progress. The world average proportion of women members of single or lower chamber legislatures is 16 per cent, with significant regional differences, as Table 10 shows. Not surprisingly the Nordic states average the highest, although similar percentages of women's representation are to be found in other European OSCE countries. Relatively high percentages of women legislators in some Sub-Saharan African countries and in Asia might be more surprising (www.ipu.org/wmn-e/classif.htm). In broad comparative terms, UK women's representation in legislatures is disappointing, but unremarkable: with just under 20 per cent, the House of Commons ranks 47th in the Inter-Parliamentary Union table of women's political representation.

TABLE 10: WOMEN IN SINGLE OR LOWER HOUSES, BY REGION	
Region	**Percentage**
Nordic	40
European OSCE countries (excluding Nordic countries)	17
Sub-Saharan Africa	17
Asia	15
Pacific	11
Arab	8

Looking beyond women's presence in legislatures, fewer that 10 per cent of cabinet members, 20 per cent of lower ranking government ministers are female and only 39 nation states have ever selected a woman as Prime Minister or President. Importantly, these low levels of women's representation are actually historic highs, achieved only after decades of struggle. They suggest an almost universal pattern of resistance to women in politics that is strongly associated with unequal and low numbers of women legislators, cabinet members and national leaders.

By concentrating on a small number of broadly similar countries, the patterns of descriptive representation outlined in Section 1 of the Report can be further analysed. This comparison brings to light two additional patterns. First, there is generally a pattern of decreasing numbers of women as political hierarchies are ascended and, second, women politicians tend to be concentrated in a narrower range of political specialisms than men.

These 'ladders of presence' map onto two overlapping hierarchies of political position. The first runs between the grass roots of local politics through regional levels of representation to central governments, cabinets, Prime Ministers and Presidents. The second is a hierarchy of function whereby certain cabinet portfolios, legislative committee positions and leadership of public bodies are traditionally considered to be more powerful and important than others. Both hierarchies are gendered: in most countries there are greater numbers of women serving in local or regional institutions than in national legislatures, although there are exceptions. [46] Moreover, a functional division of labour between women and men representatives exists whereby women are more likely to specialise in 'soft' and less prestigious policy areas such as health, cultural affairs, education and social welfare while men dominate the traditionally more prestigious areas of economic management, foreign affairs and home affairs. Paradoxically, and too often overlooked, is the fact that these 'soft' policy areas in which women are more likely to be found constitute the major part of state activity and absorb the bulk of government budgets. These two patterns not only both raise the important question of what, if any, influence women representatives have and where and how they are able to exercise it, but they also suggest at the ways in which the inclusion of women is potentially transformative of politics. In particular, women's prioritisation of social issues may, as their presence increases, push social policy onto and further up the political agenda.

To examine the inclusion of women and women's concerns and perspectives in both hierarchies of politics we look first at comparative research on the determinants of women's political recruitment, second at strategies to enhance representation and thirdly at research on the impact of women representatives.

Explaining women's political recruitment

The standard comparative research finding on women's political representation shows that institutional/procedural, social, cultural and political factors affect levels of representation. Institutional factors include rules and procedures of eligibility, electoral and party systems and legislative arrangements. Social factors include women's levels of employment and education and the division of labour in the family. Cultural factors include beliefs about appropriate gender roles in relation to politics and to the public sphere more generally. One recent study reduces these to variations in patterns of religious belief (Inglehart and Norris 2003).

As outlined in Section 1 of this Report, the supply and demand model of political recruitment suggests that countries with broadly similar social and cultural systems should see similar patterns of women's numerical representation. Yet, by examining patterns of women's representation in Western Europe and the Anglo American democracies with similar socio-cultural patterns - and despite important gains in women's social and economic status in recent years - dramatically different percentages of women in parliament are evident, ranging from 11.5 per cent in Italy to 45 per cent in Sweden. Even if we exclude the Nordic states, the variation is still significant with the Netherlands at 37 per cent.

Table 11 illustrates the changes in women's political representation in 12 comparable democracies since 1945. It shows that women's representation in national legislatures has increased in all 12 countries. However, both the timing and extent of the increases differ significantly. Finland, Norway and Sweden illustrate the Nordic pattern. In these countries, the proportion of women legislators rose dramatically in the

1970s - a decade earlier than in the Netherlands and two decades earlier than elsewhere. Two countries, Sweden and Finland, had significant increases of women representatives in each post-war decade.

TABLE 11: CHANGES IN THE PERCENTAGE OF WOMEN SELECTED TO NATIONAL LEGISLATURES (LOWER OR SINGLE CHAMBERS) SINCE 1945

	1945 [A]	1955	1965	1975	1985	1995	2005
Austria	5.5	6.3	6.7	6.0	9.3	25.1	33.9
Belgium	1.4	4.2	3.3	6.6	7.5	12.0	34.7
Finland	8.5	15.0	13.5	23.0	31.0	33.5	37.5
France	5.5	3.5	1.7	1.6	5.9	6.1	12.2
Germany [B]	6.9 [C]	8.8	6.9	5.8	9.8	26.3	32.8
Italy	3.8 [D]	5.6	4.6	3.9	7.9	15.1	11.5
Netherlands	4.0 [D]	4.0	6.7	5.3	18.7	22.7	36.7
Norway	4.7	6.7	8.0	23.3	34.4	39.4	38.2
Spain	-	-	-	-	6.3	15.7	36.0
Sweden	7.8	12.2	13.3	21.1	29.5	40.4	45.3
UK	3.8	3.8	4.6	4.3	3.5	9.2	19.7
USA Senate	0	1.0	2.0	0	2.0	9.0	14.0
USA HR	2.5	2.7	2.8	3.7	5.0	11.0	15.2

[A] 1945 or first post-WW2 election
[B] Federal Republic of Germany to 1990
[C] 1949
[D] 1946

Note: Data are for most recent election.
Source: Compiled from Lovenduski *et.al.* (Ed) State Feminism and the Political representation of Women. Cambridge University Press. 2005. Inter Parliamentary Union (www.ipu.org/wmn-e/classif.htm)

Although a number of factors explain the differences between the countries represented in Table 11, the best-established finding, borne out by the table, is that women fare best in proportional electoral systems. All the early starters and higher levels of women's political representation were achieved in countries with proportional electoral systems. The three countries in Table 11 with majoritarian electoral systems - France, the UK and the USA - were amongst the latest starters and achieved the least progress.

While there are almost as many electoral systems as there are countries in Table 11, many differences are matters of detail. Broadly speaking, there are two main types of electoral system– majoritarian and proportional. Majoritarian systems include simple plurality systems, second ballot and alternative vote systems. Proportional systems include the additional member and party list systems. Three main aspects of electoral systems may affect women's representation:

1 The ballot structure

2 List or single candidate, district magnitude or the number of seats per district

3 The level of proportionality in the allocation of votes to seats (see Norris 1993 for full discussion and bibliography

Advocates of women's greater political representation have long been aware that majoritarian, and especially the 'first past the post' single member constituency system of election is unfavourable to women's representation. In contrast, women often benefit from proportional representation party list systems for the following reasons:

1 Parties presenting lists have an incentive to present socially balanced slates of candidates to the electorate

2 Incumbency effects are slightly weaker, thus a few more vacancies are generated

3 Party lists facilitate equality guarantees because they offer more opportunities to include women without excluding men, while in single member constituencies where parties may nominate only one candidate, parties must choose between women and men candidates

The core argument here is that where parties must field only one candidate they will opt for the safest nomination, normally a middle class, middle aged white male. However, where parties may nominate a number of candidates for a particular constituency they will have an incentive to appear diverse – to 'look' more representative - and thus will be more likely to include a variety of types of candidates. In these circumstances it is likely to be easier for equality advocates to put pressure on parties to nominate women or members of ethnic or other minorities.

Importantly, proportional representation systems may facilitate but do not guarantee women's presence. Not all countries with PR have higher levels of women representatives than those with majoritarian systems. In the absence of pressure to increase the numbers of women nominated in PR systems, it is likely that their numbers will remain low. Nonetheless, in general, women have achieved higher levels of political representation earlier in proportional than in majoritarian systems.

In the first section of this Report we argue that demand-side factors offer the most convincing explanation for women's under representation at Westminster. In so doing, supply-side factors are not dismissed out of hand. Indeed, they are a key determinant of the kinds of women who put themselves forward for selection. However, we noted that relatively high levels of women's education and employment, and a steady increase of women in the brokerage occupations that are compatible with public life, decreasing family size, improving health, longer life expectancies and so forth, had not translated into similar increases in political representation. This pattern contrasts with the experience in the Nordic states where incremental changes in women's social position were associated with increases in their political representation. Part of the reason for this difference lies in the high threshold of representation for Westminster. However, the other main obstacle at Westminster – in particular, the critical role political parties play in selecting women for winnable seats – is more widespread.

Recently Nordic scholars have revisited the arguments about the relationship between supply- and demand-side theories of women's representation. Danish political scientist Drude Dahlerup argues that there are two tracks to equality in women's numerical representation – the incremental and the fast track. In the incremental track, small and gradual improvements in women's socio-economic position may lead, eventually, to parity between women and men in politics. In this conceptualisation, women are content to wait for equality through decades of gradual change. Such an incremental track took place in the equality minded Nordic states and the Netherlands.

Case Study:

The Incremental Track

Political parties in Denmark, Norway and Sweden used quota provisions in the 1980s to increase women's political representation. By that time women were already between 20 and 30 per cent of legislators. So, although the introduction of quotas led to further increases, a significant breakthrough had already taken place (Dahlerup and Friedenvall 2003). In these countries equality promotion had led to the building of political capacity so that women, once elected, were able to operate effectively, not least to promote further increases in the political representation of women.

The incremental track is, seemingly, no longer an option. Globally, women are claiming their right to political representation and demanding quotas to secure it without waiting for secularisation to take place, or welfare states to develop, or for periods of democratic stability, to make gradual increases in presence possible. In the 'fast track' approach, equality guarantees are used to jump-start the equality process by placing women in positions of power and authority, altering recruitment mechanisms accordingly. The rationale underpinning this alternative approach is that women's exclusion from politics itself is the problem; inclusion is the obvious solution (Dahlerup and Friedenvall 2003).

Quotas: the Fast Track

Throughout the world, the use of fast track strategies has increased since the 1980s and measures such as quotas have now been used in more than 90 countries. Frequently such measures are adopted in democratising systems. The examples of South Africa, where ANC women demanded and obtained quotas so that over 30 per cent of the founding legislature were women, and of Latin America, where democratising parties have established quotas of women, are cases in point.

The use of quotas is also common in the democracies considered here where political parties are the major players. In most of the 12 systems in Table 11 at least some political parties have implemented quotas. In two countries, France and Belgium, legal quotas of women were established in the 1990s, while in the USA only 'soft' quotas have been used and only for internal party offices. Only rarely do all the political parties in a system adopt quotas and in systems of legal quotas the parties vary in the effectiveness of their implementation. At one time associated with the left, there are now many examples of centre and right wing parties adopting quotas of women candidates (Guadagnini 2005, Norris 2003). In Italy, for example, politicians from the extreme right, notably the Fascist Alessandra Mussolini, have advocated quotas (Guadagnini 2005). But the central point remains – it is political parties which determine the levels of women's political representation.

Comparative research suggests that the institutional and cultural context, the type of electoral and party system, affects not only the kind of quotas that are adopted but also their likelihood of being implemented (see Box 4 in Section 1). The success of the Labour Party in introducing quotas in the UK notwithstanding, it is normally more difficult to use a fast track strategy in majoritarian political systems than in proportional systems. Closed lists and high district magnitude favour effective implementation thereby delivering more women representatives (Htun and Jones 2003). However, favourable institutional settings alone do not guarantee better political representation of women; Quotas are present in political systems with high, medium and low levels of women's political representation (Krook 2003). Implementation depends upon party compliance, which in turn depends on normative attitudes towards women's numerical representation and the calculations that leaders make about the benefits of compliance in relation to the costs of non-compliance. In short, whether quotas constitute in practice equality rhetoric, equality promotion or equality guarantees depends upon the details of their requirements and particularly upon the sanctions that are used in the event of non-compliance (Dahlerup and Freidenvall 2003).

The detail of quota provision matters for their effectiveness, not least because political parties are generally not enthusiastic quota implementers. The reluctance of political parties to implement the quotas was one of the major barriers to their effectiveness in Bolivia and Brazil, for example, where 30 per cent quotas have so far led to representations of women in national legislatures of 19 and 12 per cent respectively (Krook 2003; Araújo 2003; Benavides 2003). Thus, even where quotas are adopted, they may well not be fully implemented, as the cases of both Belgium and France reveal: in Belgium, disappointing results in the first parity elections led to rule changes and the expansion of sanctions to improve the results of the next round (Meier 2005); similarly the parity law in France did not, in itself, guarantee increases in women's political representation.

Case Study:

Legal quotas in Belgium

In Belgium an initial quota of 33.3 per cent was not met because political parties did not place women in winnable positions on their lists. They followed the letter and not the spirit of the quota law. In the light of these shortcomings, the parliament raised the quota to 50 per cent and added further stipulations to the regulations whereby the first two candidates on a party list must not be members of the same sex. However, the stipulations applied only to the top positions and other changes in electoral law had mixed effects on the effectiveness of the legal quotas, hence the subsequent election returned 35.3 per cent of women legislators – an improvement on the previous election but still short of the 50 per cent requirement (Meier 2005).

Case Study:

Parity Law in France

The parity law, a 50 per cent quota, led to little change in the presence of women in the French National Assembly and to disappointing, albeit much improved, results in local elections. The strength of the parity law varies by the level of election in France, which has a mix of proportional and majoritarian electoral systems. In the regional and local proportional systems parties were required to place women in high list position. Failure to do so resulted in the strong sanction of being unable to contest the election. However, in the national majoritarian elections, sanctions were financial and larger parties especially were able to ignore them. Thus the post-parity elections led to considerable, but far short of parity, increases in sub national elections but almost no increase in the numbers of women in the National Assembly (Murray 2005).

The democratising systems of Eastern and Central Europe offer an even stronger counter example. As elsewhere, quotas are more or less avoidable at implementation stage, not all parties adopt quotas and not all of those which do utilise them fully. In Eastern and Central Europe the routine inclusion of substantial percentages of women in powerless legislatures by the discredited former regimes left campaigners for women's presence in politics without an acceptable strategy for implementing their claims during crucial post-transition elections (Matland and Montgomery 2003). Later, quotas were adopted in Bosnia and Herzegovina, Croatia, Hungary, Poland, Romania, Slovakia, and Slovenia (www.idea.etc.) although with varying levels of success in terms of increasing women's political representation. The reintroduction of quotas in East Central Europe are attributed to 'design borrowing' by parties of particular institutions found in sister parties in Western Europe; women's mobilisations; and because of an association between modernisation with feminisation in systems where some political parties compete on the basis of their contributions to transition and modernisation (Matland 2003). However, while, as elsewhere, the significant variations in women's political representation in post-Communist systems have complex explanations, it is political parties that make the crucial recruitment decisions.

The Politics of Quotas

The arguments that support quotas are context specific, affected by the discourses and cultures of the systems in which arguments must be made. Arguments for quotas are often framed as practical matters that invite pragmatic considerations and their appearance is associated with electoral cycles, party fortunes and constitutional change. Male party leaders often agree to the implementation of quotas for mainly strategic electoral reasons, notably to appeal to women voters.

In many countries quotas are adopted as symbols of democratic representation in what are otherwise less than democratic states. CEDAW[47] has been important to such decisions; hence quotas have been implemented in systems in which women do not have equal social rights. In 2001 Pakistan introduced 33 per cent quotas for women at municipal level. In some Arab countries the quota system is used to get token and controllable women on board while claiming that they promote women's representation. In Uganda one parliamentary seat from each of 39 districts is reserved for women. In Argentina, electoral law established a 30 per cent quota for candidates. In South Africa, women (mainly ANC women) pushed for quotas and a substantial presence in the legislature, yet women workers have been raped in the parliament building (Dahlerup 2002).

Pragmatic considerations are often important in decisions by male dominated parties to introduce quotas. They may wish to make a claim that they represent women and require quotas as a symbolic means of demonstrating their commitment to meeting that obligation. They may be responding to the claims of party members who have come to see the importance of quotas if change is to occur (2005). They may also adopt quotas for electoral reasons: Carlos Mennen supported quotas when he thought he would lose an election if he did not. Many East European regimes, having rejected quotas in the early stages of democratisation, later returned to them, in part because alliances with West European countries made it politically attractive to meet claims for women's representation. Such 'contagion effects' in modern democracies are, once again, most likely to be found in proportional systems (Matland and Studlar 1996).

Above all, though, quotas are political strategies. They do not come into being by accident and they do not guarantee the election of feminist politicians, as the election of Front National women in France vividly demonstrates. Whatever the context however, women's agency is critical to decisions to adopt quotas. The achievement of increased women's political representation rarely takes place without a political struggle in which equality advocates must both mobilise and take advantage of the available opportunities. Party women's organisations, feminist movements and women's interest groups have become skilled at demanding quotas to achieve increases in women's political representation. To introduce quotas against severe resistance '...requires that women have already gained some power' (Dahlerup 1998).

Does it matter? The Comparative Evidence

As Section 2 of this Report made clear, simplistic assumptions about the relationship between women's descriptive and substantive representation or between the proportions of women present in legislatures and their effect are unhelpful. The best research on the relationship between the substantive and descriptive political representation of women examines the behaviour of women representatives in the context in which it takes place.

In the same way that research on the behaviour of women representatives at Westminster and elsewhere may not be conclusive, even if it is consistent, scholars looking at a range of different political institutions have found that the presence of a significant number of women legislators is associated with changes in procedures, culture, language and the agenda of a parliament. Women politicians are more likely than their male colleagues to involve themselves in the promotion of women's concerns (Carroll 1985; Vallance and Davies 1986; Duerst-Lahti and Kelly 1995). Other studies confirm findings from UK institutions that suggest that women may have a different political style. The 1995 collection of essays about legislators in the USA, edited by Georgia Duerst-Lahti and

Rita Mae Kelly, offers a wealth of evidence that political style is gendered (Duerst-Lahti and Kelly 1995). Survey and interview evidence also indicates that women politicians prefer the politics of problem solving, policy development and service delivery to the politics of confrontation. Studies also suggest that women place a higher priority on social issues that relate to family, children and women than do men (Norris 1987; Thomas 1994).

One of the earliest research projects on the impact of women representatives in actually existing legislatures was, for obvious reasons, undertaken on the Scandinavian systems. In her seminal study of critical acts by Scandinavian women legislators, Drude Dahlerup found that increases in the presence of women legislators were associated with changes in the political agenda, especially in respect of sex equality issues, changes in the political discourse and in the behaviour and priorities of male legislators (Dahlerup 1988). While issues of women's concern traditionally had low priority in the legislatures and were rarely taken up by men, such issues were addressed by women representatives. Later studies of Scandinavian systems generally supported and extended Dahlerup's findings. A Norwegian study in the early 1990s found that traditional party differences continued to be expressed in the activities and interventions of women legislators with conservative women advocating policies to support women's traditional family roles while women on the left pursued policies to enhance women's access to employment markets and public life more generally (Skjeie 1993).

Case study:
Norway
Norwegian MPs were asked whether they believed that men and women party members held different political interests or viewpoints.

The question was open-ended, and specifications depended solely on the respondents' own perceptions. The politicians thought that women's interests mainly included social and welfare policies, environmental protection, equality policies, disarmament policies and educational policies. By contrast, men's interests included economic and industrial policies, energy issues, transportation, national security and foreign affairs. According to the researchers, the structure of gender interests reported by politicians were categorical: there was no overlap reported in men's and women's interests. Thus the study suggested that the majority of the Norwegian political elite, both men and women, had internalised conceptualisations of male and female areas of political concern. The research concluded that in Norwegian politics at that time, a mandate of difference was attached to women politicians. It was used by women themselves to get inside the power institutions, and was recognised by the party leadership, both men and women, as a relevant political mandate (Skjeie 2002).

The balance of the available evidence is that women and men politicians differ and that women are likely to intervene to place women's concerns on the political agenda. More tangentially, there is some evidence that the presence of women legislators strengthens democracy by increasing the political participation of women. For example, in Britain in 2001, women's voting turnout was four per cent higher than men's in seats in which a woman was elected to Parliament. Moreover, women reported that they were more interested in the electoral campaign and more likely to be active in the campaign in seats where a woman MP was elected (Norris, Lovenduski and Campbell 2004). Similar results were found in American studies (Burns, Schlozman and Verba 2001).

Case Study:

Feminising the Swedish Riksdag

Drawing on interview data with successive cohorts of Swedish legisla-tors, Wängnerud concludes that women's presence in the Riksdag brought about a shift of emphasis in politics whereby women's interests became more central. She found differences in attitudes between women and men across a range of issues and showed that women MPs have affected the policy agenda both by bringing to it issues such as gender equality, which are rarely promoted by men, and also by giving higher priority to social policies especially care and family policies than men (Budapest symposium 2005). She also established that these dif-ferences provoked political changes that led to an increased legislative sensitivity to women's interests by all politicians (Wängnerud 2000).

Other research reports that the attitudes of women and men gradual-ly converge as the numbers of women increase. This, and similar find-ings might alarm sex equality advocates who fear that such a conver-gence (the absence of sex differences) might mean that women were becoming more like men. Yet, close examination and consideration of generational change indicates that attitude and behavioural change affects both sexes who are adapting to new modes of doing politics (Karvonnen and Per Selle 1995; Lovenduski 2005; Sones et al 2005). Moreover, recent research gives further reasons for optimism and counters the fear that women representatives have been assimilated. Mateo Diaz found evidence that, as the balance between men's and women's presence is achieved, women representatives have more influence on the attitudes and preferences of men politicians than the other way around (Mateo Diaz 2002). Such findings add to a growing body of evidence that one of the things that changes as the numbers of women change is men. This suggests that the process of achieving women's presence both generates and is part of a wider reconsideration of gender roles. Thus, new patterns of political behaviour should become evident whereby not only do women and men politicians *become* more similar, but also, as generations shift, politics attracts and recruits men and women who *are* more similar in attitudes and social characteristics both to each other and to their electorates.

Case Study:
The Recruitment of Women in Belgium and Sweden

Where women's presence remains below or around 15 to 20 per cent of the legislature, women MPs are less like women voters than male MPs are like men voters in terms of their social characteristics. It is the recruitment process that causes this difference. When women are recruited, they have to display male qualifications; hence they will tend to have social characteristics more likely to be found among men. For example they may have careers in male dominated professions such as business or law. Alternatively, they may have sacrificed their domestic lives in order to compete in male dominated arenas and thus would share social characteristics with neither women nor men. For example, they may be less statistically likely to marry or to have children either than other women or men. However, as the proportion of women nears parity, it becomes more likely that women are selected because of their gender rather than despite their sex, hence they are more likely to reflect the social characteristics of women in the electorate (Mateo Diaz 2002).

[46] Since the 1970s there has been no difference and in the 1980s more women were elected to parliament than to local councils in Sweden. Other exceptions are the Netherlands, Finland and Norway.

[47] Convention on the Elimination of Discrimination Against Women adopted by the UN General Assembly in 1979.

Conclusion and Recommendations

Understanding women's political representation

Women's under-representation in politics is a global phenomenon, averaging just 16 per cent in national legislatures. Yet, there is no single explanation: socio-economic, cultural and political determinants combine in different ways to account for the numbers of women elected to a particular legislature. Cross-national comparisons reveal widely differing economic, social and political structures and cultures and similar numbers of women representatives as well as countries with similar economic, social and political structures and culture and widely differing numbers of women representatives.

In the past it was thought that as women's social, economic and cultural position changed over time the levels of women's representation would correspondingly improve - the 'incremental track'. However, there is now an emergent consensus that the barriers to women's greater political representation have more to do with the workings of politics *per se* than wider societal or structural features. Since the 1990s, many countries have taken a 'fast track' to women's greater representation through the use of equality guarantees that ensure the inclusion of women. In many instances it is the use of sex quotas, often combined with the use of proportional electoral systems, that explains the variable rates of women's political representation across institutions and countries.

Women's political representation in British politics: the case for equality guarantees

At the 2005 general election, 128 women were elected to the House of Commons, constituting 20 per cent of all MPs, a small increase from the 2001 election, but still a long way from parity. In the global rankings of national legislatures Westminster is placed 47th and compares unfavourably, following the 2003 elections, with the National Assembly for Wales where women constitute 50 per cent of the Assembly Members and the Scottish Parliament where 40 per cent of the MSPs are female. The lack of ethnic diversity amongst current women MPs, MSPs and AMs is also a notable feature of women's political representation in the UK: there are only two Black women MPs and no BME women (or men for that matter) sitting in either Edinburgh or Cardiff.

Furthermore, the recent increases in the numbers of women at Westminster and, indeed, elsewhere in the UK, are party specific and reliant upon the use of equality guarantees: Labour women constitute 77 per cent of all women MPs elected in 2005 and more than half of all Labour women MPs currently sitting in Parliament were selected on All Women Shortlists in either 1997 or 2005. The other parties at Westminster have seen only incremental change in the numbers of women MPs over the last decade and in proportional terms the Conservative Party is currently flat-lining.

The opportunity to follow a 'fast track' to women's political representation through the use of equality guarantees has been available to all political parties since 2002. The Sex Discrimination (Election Candidates) Act permits their use for elections to Westminster, the devolved institutions, European elections and local government elections. Yet, with the Conservative Party opposed to, and the Liberal

Democrats divided over the issue, only the Labour Party took up the opportunity and re-introduced its policy of All Women Shortlists (AWS) for the 2005 general election. The other parties relied upon equality rhetoric and equality promotion.

However, as this Report demonstrates, equality rhetoric and equality promotion produce only very gradual improvements in the representation of women. Any significant future change would appear to be reliant upon the use of equality guarantees by *all* political parties. Long-held, and in some cases, heartfelt, opposition to equality guarantees should be reconsidered. They may not be 'fair', they may grate against liberal principles, they may, as critics claim, cast aspersions on the merit of the women elected, but one thing cannot be denied, measures that *guarantee* women's election work, and work quickly.

With the Sex Discrimination (EC) Act expiring in 2015 (it has a sunset clause), it is incumbent on the political parties to support the necessary secondary legislation to ensure its continuation. Advocates of women's political representation also need to address the failure of all parties to select (via equality guarantees or not), and elect, a diverse group of women MPs. The House of Commons, it should be remembered, remains an overwhelmingly white as well as male space.

Making a difference and acting for women

Proving a direct causal relationship between the presence of women (women's descriptive representation) and feminised change (the integration of women's concerns and perspectives into politics) is nigh on impossible. Rejecting the simplistic - and highly misleading - concept of critical mass as an explanation for when women in politics are likely to effect a feminisation of politics, this Report favours reframing the question to *how* the substantive representation of women occurs.

Through the presentation of case studies from the UK and comparison countries, this Report demonstrates that there is highly suggestive and consistent evidence of women making a difference to politics and acting for women. In the UK, the case studies reveal that there are sex differences in attitudes between women and men representatives, particularly in respect of attitudes towards women's concerns, as well as instances of different parliamentary behaviour. There is also evidence that women in the 1997 and 2001 parliaments had a feminised effect on legislation, with the case studies of the Sex Discrimination (EC) Act and reducing VAT on sanitary products. Finally, there are indications that women and men at Westminster, Edinburgh and Cardiff agree that there are different gendered styles of politics.

Notwithstanding the presentation of a clear case that the election of greater numbers of women in politics effects feminised change, this Report does not make the case for women's presence on this basis, justice arguments are alone sufficient. Linking women's presence in parliament and substantive representation of women's interests and concerns can be important to mobilise women's political participation, and higher levels of women's representation are symbolically valuable. However, we argue that women's equal political representation is necessary for the simple reason of justice; any additional substantive benefits are to be welcomed but women's presence should not be premised upon them.

Recommendations

In order to deliver more representative political institutions in the UK:

1   Political parties should support the principle of equal political representation of women and men *(equality rhetoric)*; they should encourage women from a diversity of socio-economic and ethnic backgrounds to seek political office

2   Political parties should ensure selection processes are non-discriminatory; to this end they should employ *equality promotion* measures, for example, gender - and Black and Minority Ethnic - (BME) sensitive training for party selection committees and party members

3   Political parties should operate internal sex quotas for party positions which helps to deliver a larger pool of potential candidates for election

4   Political parties should act to eliminate sexual harassment in their parties and set a good example in terms of sex-balanced staff appointments

5   Political parties should act to ensure, not only the selection but also, the election of equal numbers of women and men by selecting women for winnable contests

6   Political parties should employ measures that *guarantee* parity of representation and recognise that, in the absence of these, there will be only limited and incremental change and that this is unacceptable

7   Political parties should monitor their selection procedures using equality trained monitors and produce reports on the outcomes of their selection processes after each election

8   The Government should consider introducing prescriptive rather than permissive legislation; at the minimum, the Government should, along with the other political parties, actively support the extension by secondary legislation of the Sex Discrimination (Election Candidates) Act that permits the use of equality guarantees and which expires in 2015

9   The Government should implement international protocols and treaties requiring equality of women's representation

10 The Government should provide funding for political parties to institute, operate and monitor equality selection procedures

11 The Government should fund research on equal representation

12 Westminster should learn the lessons from Scotland and Wales and reform itself to be more family-friendly and take more seriously work-life balance as one factor that determines who seeks elected political office in the UK

13 Arguments of justice and fairness should be used in support of women's political representation; although women can make a difference and act for women, their political presence should not be dependent upon so doing.

Afterword

Having struggled to gain the right to vote and stand for office, the suffragettes assumed that political power would follow. How wrong they were.

In her book *Feminising Politics*, Joni Lovenduski gives an idea of what it was like for Nancy Astor, the first woman to take her seat in the House of Commons in 1919. She is said to have told her son that 'if I had known how much men would hate it, I would never have dared do it'.

Margaret Wintringham, the second woman to take her seat, had a similar experience. She was said to have 'found the feeling of hatred she experienced when she went into the House to be so great that if Nancy Astor was not present in the chamber at the same time, the atmosphere was so unbearable she had to leave'.

Having been elected in 2001, I can say that things have improved since those early days. This is to be expected but just how much progress have we made? Like the proverbial curate's egg, this report from the Hansard Society confirms that it is only good in parts.

The first and most obvious point to make is that there are still not nearly enough women in the House of Commons – only 127 of us out of the 646 MPs elected in May 2005. In other words, just under 20 per cent, giving us a ranking of 47th in the Inter-Parliamentary Union table of women's political representation. There have only ever been 291 women MPs – significantly fewer than the current 519 male MPs.

However disappointing, that figure still represents substantial progress over the last 25 years. The Labour Party's use of All Women Shortlists in 1997 saw the number of women MPs double. Legal challenges led to an ending of the policy and a subsequent dip in women MPs in 2001. The Government moved quickly to introduce the Sex Discrimination (Election Candidates) Act 2002 to allow political parties to discriminate positively in favour of women. However, it is only the Labour Party that has been successful in significantly increasing its percentage of women MPs with 65 per cent of the new intake of Labour MPs being women – the first time ever that women have outnumbered men.

It is a real shame that other parties are making so little progress because ultimately it affects the democratic process and we all lose out. As the Report shows, more women than men turned out to vote in 2001 in seats in which a woman was elected. Women were also more active in campaigns in seats where a woman was ultimately elected.

The Report tells us that having more women legislators can lead to changes in procedures, culture, language and the agenda of the parliament itself. There is no doubt that women politicians place a higher priority than men on social issues that relate to family, children and women.

In my experience, far more women than men ask questions about women's employment, domestic violence, childcare, equal pay and women's health. This, in turn, can lead to an increased legislative sensitivity to women's interests by all politicians. I've seen the difference over the last eight years with, for example, a huge increase in the provision of childcare and new legislation on domestic violence. Encouragingly the Report tells us that research shows that the attitudes of men and women gradually converge as the numbers of women in political office increase.

All of this begs a question. Why are there still so few women in Parliament, almost a century after we forced male political society to take account of us? In particular, why are there so few black and minority ethnic women?

The answer, as the Report says, has more to do with the way our political system operates than anything else. As many of us have argued for years, the problem is not so much an issue of supply, as one of demand.

There are more than enough women, able and willing to do the job. However they face a range of barriers in getting there, not least discrimination by the political parties' selection processes. The report tells us that the three main parties selected over 400 women as parliamentary candidates at the last election. The number of candidates willing to stand is clearly not the issue. The trouble was that not nearly enough of them were selected to stand in winnable seats.

Of course it's not just in politics that women are under-represented. The Government understands that barriers face women in all walks of life and this underpinned our successful campaign last year to improve diversity in the boardroom. We talked to the chairs of literally dozens of FTSE 100 companies, and convinced them that if they wanted more women in the boardroom then they needed to think far more laterally than they had done in the past. We advised them to look critically at the criteria they applied to directors' posts and, crucially, to consider ways of widening the pool from which they traditionally recruited. Many are now doing just that.

This approach is bearing fruit, as did our campaign a couple of years ago to encourage more women to join the boards of national public bodies. We made contact with thousands of women already active in public life as school governors and magistrates, and gave them practical advice about how to raise their game. As part of that campaign, the Government set a target to increase the numbers of women appointed to public bodies by 50 per cent. Every Government department now has an action plan to help translate that principle into practice.

That is not to say that supply-side factors are not an issue. I am only too aware that women are, on average, poorer than men; not just in terms of resources. Women are more likely to be the carers in family life with less time to engage in politics and may have less confidence in their abilities to get on. In Parliament a return to another late night sitting was viewed with dismay by many women MPs and aspiring politicians.

Things are far from perfect, we can and should do more to remove barriers to women's participation in every area of life but this extremely comprehensive report helps to clarify that the issue is one of demand. It should, therefore, be compulsory reading for all political party members involved in selecting their candidate as, in many ways, they hold the key to the future of fair representation.

Meg Munn MP
Deputy Minister for Women and Equality
October 2005

APPENDIX 1

Updating the 2000 *Women at the Top* Report: Women's representation in the professions and public life

The following précis provide a brief overview on the situation of women in the professions and public life, updating the previous *Women at the Top* Reports.

Public Appointments
There has been an increase in the percentage of women holding national public appointments. In 1994 women held 30 per cent, they now hold 34 per cent. During 2001-2002, 39 per cent of new and re-appointments were women. However, BME women hold just 1.8 per cent of national public appointments. [1]

The Civil Service
In 2004, women made up 52.3 per cent of civil service staff and 25.8 per cent of the senior civil service level (SCS level). There has been an increase of 8.6 per cent in the representation of women at the SCS level since 1999, when women made up 17.2 per cent. Nonetheless, women's presence at this level varies widely by department: women constituted 38 per cent at the Department of Health, 36.5 per cent in the ODPM and the DfES but only 8.2 per cent at the Ministry of Defence and 12.9 per cent of FCO senior staff. Women were better represented in the Treasury at 26.2 per cent. [2]

The Judiciary

As Table 1 shows, there has been some improvement in the position of women in the judiciary. Most high profile is the appointment of Lord Justice Brenda Hale who was appointed in October 2003 as one of the 12 Lords of Appeal in Ordinary, who sit in the House of Lords. There have also been modest improvements in the number of women sitting as High Court Judges, Circuit Judges and as Recorders.

TABLE 1: THE JUDICIARY				
	1989		2005	
Judicial Office	Total	% Women	Total	% Women
Law Lords	10	0	12	8
Lord Justices	27	4	37	5
High Court Judges	81	1	96	9
Circuit Judges	434	4	490	10
Recorders	703	5	1108	13

Source: 2000 *Women at the Top* Report and DCA website. [3]

Legal Profession

In 2004, women represented 40 per cent of solicitors and 30 per cent of barristers, but only eight per cent of Queen's Counsel. [4] With respect to the latter, and despite increases in the percentages of women applying for Silk between 1995 and 2000 (from 8.5 per cent to 10.5 per cent), by 2003 the percentage had fallen back to 9.9 per cent. Moreover, in each of these years, women constituted 11.3 per cent, 12.8 per cent and 7.4 per cent of those awarded Silk, respectively. In other areas of the law women fare better: in 2004 women constituted 67 per cent of the Crown Prosecution Service workforce: 27 per cent of the Senior Civil Servants and 22 per cent of Chief Crown Prosecutors. [5]

As indicated in the main Report, issues of equal opportunities have been identified in and by the professions and business. The legal profession is a good example of this: the Commission for Judicial Appointments has identified systematic bias in the way the judiciary and the legal professions operate – noting 'narrow and inappropriate views about who is suited for appointment'; [6] the Bar Council now requires all barristers' chambers to formalise their policies on maternity leave; responsibility [7] for the 'quality mark' for Silk appointments has been given to the Bar Council and Law Society; [8] and the Fawcett Society has investigated the legal profession's gender pay gap. [9]

Police Service

Women now represent 20 per cent of all police officers but there are only four women out of 43 Chief Constables (9.3 per cent), an improvement from the 2000 report when 6.4 per cent of Chief Constables were women. Recently Patricia Gallan became the first BME woman ever appointed at the Assistant Chief Police Officer (ACPO) level. [10]

Higher Education

There has been a sharp increase in the number of female academics in UK higher education over the last two decades.[11] However, women's jobs are less senior and more casualised than their male colleagues - in 2002-3, 48 per cent of women and 38 per cent of men were on fixed term contracts (see Table 2 overleaf).

TABLE 2: WOMEN IN HIGHER EDUCATION BY SENIOR APPOINTMENT, 1995-2004						
	1995/96		1998/99		2003/4	
Post	Total	% Women	Total	% Women	Total	% Women
Professors	8,649	8.6	10,261	9.8	13,525	15.1
Senior Lecturers and Researchers	16,050	8.3	19,599	21.9	24,740	28.9
Total	24,699	8.4	29,860	17.7	38,265	24

Source: Higher Education Statistics Agency individualised returns.

The Media

In 2000, the Hansard Society Report stated that no women ran major media such as newspapers or TV companies. As of 2004, women constitute 9.1 per cent of editors of national newspapers [12] and make up 4.3 per cent of Chief Executives of Media Companies.[13] The current BBC Board of Governors and Executive Board have 25 per cent and 30 per cent female membership respectively. Women constitute 23.2 per cent of the Parliamentary press gallery (which has 211 members of whom 49 are women) and 18 per cent (27) of the 150 - member Lobby. [14]

Corporate World

There may be some indications of change in women's favour at the top of the corporate world: in 2004 women made up 9.7 per cent of Directors in FTSE 100 companies (executive and non-executive directors). This is a small increase of 1.1 per cent from 2003 although latest figures show that women took 17 per cent of new director appointments.

[1] Women and Equality Unit, Women in Pubic Life: Key Facts.

[2] http://www.civilservice.gov.uk/management/information/statistical information/statistics/images/report 2004.

[3] DCA: www.dca.gov.uk/judicial/womjudfr.htm

[4] Taken from Commission on Women and the Criminal Justice System, One Year On, (Fawcett Society; London, 2005).

[5] Taken from Commission on Women and the Criminal Justice System, One Year On, (Fawcett Society; London, 2005).

[6] Commission for Judicial Appointments Annual Reports 2003 and 2004.

[7] The Economist (4 June 2005 'Sex Changes').

[8] Taken from Commission on Women and the Criminal Justice System, One Year On, (Fawcett Society; London, 2005). In another case, the EOC have suggested that in order to meet the 50 per cent target for women in public appointments headhunters commissioned to act for Government should focus on the diversity of their candidate list, or risk losing their preferred contractor status (EOC, Sex and Power: Who Runs Britain? 2005).

[9] Taken from Commission on Women and the Criminal Justice System, One Year On, (Fawcett Society; London, 2005).

[10] Taken from Commission on Women and the Criminal Justice System, One Year On, (Fawcett Society; London, 2005).

[11] www.aut.org.uk

[12] EOC, Sex and Power: Who Runs Britain? (2005) – statistics taken from Vacher's Parliamentary Companion, Sept 2004.

[13] EOC, Sex and Power: Who Runs Britain? (2005) – statistics taken from London Stock Exchange website and companies' websites, Sept 2004.

[14] Statistics drawn from information on the Parliamentary Press Gallery Site: www.thepressgallery.co.uk, 31 Aug 2005.

[15] Cranfield Centre for Developing Women Business Leaders, The 2004 Female FTSE Report, (Dec 2004). Taken from EOC, Sex and Power: Who Runs Britain? (2005).

[16] EOC, Sex and Power: Who Runs Britain? (2005).

APPENDIX 2

Key Features of Women's Participation and Substantive Representation in Scotland, Wales and Northern Ireland

Scottish Parliament

- Family friendly working hours

- Recognition of Scottish school holidays

- Visitors' crèche in Parliament

- Cross-party Parliamentary Group on women, serviced by EOC

- Access, consultation and participation key principles of Parliament

- Equal opportunities committee in Parliament

- Equality unit

- EO key principle of Parliament, stated priority of government – both committed to mainstreaming

- Scottish Parliament has power to encourage equal opportunities and to impose duties on public bodies to ensure they have due regard to equality legislation (nb, power to legislate to prohibit discrimination and to regulate EO is reserved to the UK Parliament)

- Memoranda accompanying executive bills must include an equal opportinities impact statement

National Assembly for Wales

- Family friendly working hours

- Recognition of Welsh school holidays

- Equal Opportunity Committee in the Assembly and Equality Policy Unit set up within the government

- A statutory equality duty is in place which requires that the Assembly and Assembly sponsored public bodies have 'due regard' for equality opportunities in all their functions

- Commitment to mainstreaming equality, including gender equality

- NAW sponsor a National Wales Women's Coalition, one of four consultative networks with equality groups

Northern Ireland

- Family friendly working hours

- An Equality Unit has been established in the Office of the First Minister and Deputy First Minister

- Northern Ireland Act 1998 created a powerful statutory duty (Section 75) placed upon all public bodies, including government departments, to have due regard to promote equality of opportunity and to draw up equality schemes. A new Northern Ireland Equality Commission is empowered to implement the duty

Source: Amended from Mackay, *et al* (undated)

BIBLIOGRAPHY

Araujo, Clara (2003) 'Quotas for Women in the Brazilian Legislative System' in IDEA *The Implementation of Quotas: Latin American Experience*, (Stockholm: IDEA).

Bellamy, Kate & Katherine Rake (2005) *Money, Money, Money: Is it still a rich man's world?*, (London: Fawcett Society).

Benavides, Jimena Costa (2003) 'Women's Political Participation in Bolivia' in *Quotas for Women in the Brazilian Legislative System* in IDEA *The Implementation of Quotas: Latin American Experience*, (Stockholm: IDEA).

Berrington, Hugh (1973) *Backbench Opinion in the House of Commons 1945-55*, (Oxford: Pergamon).

Bochel, Catherine & Jacqui Briggs (2000) 'Do Women Make a Difference', in *Politics*, 20:2, 63-68.

Burns, Nancy, Kay Schlozman & Sidney Verba (2001) *The Private Roots of Public Action,* (Cambridge, NA: Harvard University Press).

Campbell, Rosie (2006) *Gender and Voting Behaviour in Britain,* (Essex: ECPR Press)

Campbell, Rosie, Sarah Childs, & Joni Lovenduski (2006) *The Professionalisation of Politics,* Paper to be presented at the PSA Annual Conference 2006, Reading.

Carroll, Susan (1985) *Women as Candidates in American Politics,* (Bloomington, Indiana: University of Indiana Press).

Chaney, Paul (forthcoming) 'Critical Mass, Deliberation and the Substantive Representation of Women', in *Political Studies*.

Chaney, Paul (2004) 'Women and Constitutional Change in Wales', in *Regional and Federal Studies*, 14:2, 281-303.

Chaney, Paul (2003) 'The Post-Devolution Equality Agenda', in *Policy and Politics*, 32:1, 63-77.

Childs, Sarah (2004) *New Labour's Women MPs: Women Representing Women*, (London: Routledge).

Childs, Sarah (2003), 'The Sex Discrimination (Election Candidates) Act and its Implications', in *Representation*, 39:2, 83-92.

Childs, Sarah (2002) 'Competing Conceptions of Representation and the Passage of the Sex Discrimination (Election Candidates) Bill', in *Journal of Legislative Studies*, 8:3, 90-108.

Childs, Sarah & Mona Lena Krook (2005) 'The Substantive Representation of

Women: Rethinking the 'Critical Mass' Debate', Paper presented to the Annual Meeting of the APSA 2005, Washington.

Childs, Sarah & Julie Withey (2004), 'Do Women Sign for Women? Sex and the Signing of Early Day Motions in the 1997 Parliament', in *Political Studies* 52, 552-564.

Clark, Janet (1994) 'Getting There: Women in Political Office', in Marianne Githens, Pippa Norris & Joni Lovenduski (eds), *Different Roles, Different Voices* (New York: Harper Collins), 99-110.

Cockburn, Cynthia (1996), 'Strategies for Gender Democracy', in *European Journal of Women's Studies*, 3:7, 7-26.

Commission on Women & the Criminal Justice System (2005) *One Year On,* (London: Fawcett Society).

Cowell-Myers, Kimberly (2003) *Women Legislators in Northern Ireland: Gender and Politics in the New Legislative Assembly:* Occasional paper No.3. (Belfast: Centre for Advancement of Women in Politics, Queens University).

Cowley, Philip & Sarah Childs (2003) 'Too Spineless To Rebel', in *British Journal of Political Science*, 33:3, 345-65.

Dahlerup, Drude (2002) 'ECPR Research Session: Gender Quotas in a Comparative Perspective', Geneva, September 19-22.

Dahlerup, Drude (1998) 'Using quotas to increase women's political representation', in Karam, Azza (ed.) *Women in Parliament: Beyond Numbers,* (Stockholm: IDEA).

Dahlerup, Drude (1988), 'From a Small to a Large Minority', in *Scandinavia Political Studies,* 11:4, 275-99.

Dahlerup, Drude & Lenita Freidenvall (2003) 'Quotas as a fast track to equal political representation for women: why Scandinavia is no longer the model', Paper presented to the 19th International Political Science Association World Congress 2003, Durban, South Africa.

Dobrowolsky, Alexandra & Vivien Hart (2003) *Women Making Constitutions* (Basingstoke: Palgrave).

Dodson, Debra (2001) 'The Impact of Women in Congress', Paper presented to Annual Meeting of APSA Women and Politics Special Session 2001, San Francisco.

Duerst–Lahti, Georgia & Rita Mae Kelly (eds.) (1995) *Gender Power, Leadership and Governance,* (Ann Arbor: University of Michigan Press).

Edwards, Julia & Laura McAllisiter (2002) 'One Step Forward, Two Steps Back? Women in the Two Main Political Parties in Wales' in *Parliamentary Affairs:* 55:1, 154-166.

Equal Opportunities Commission (2005) *Greater Expectations: Summary Final Report, EOC's Investigation into Pregnancy Discrimination*, (Manchester: EOC).

Equal Opportunities Commission (2005) *Sex and Power: Who Runs Britain?*, (Manchester: EOC).

EOC Working Paper (2002) 'Advancing women in the workplace: case studies', http://www.eoc.org.uk/cseng/research/awiw_casestudies.pdf.

Fawcett Society (2005) *Black & Minority Ethnic Women in the UK*, (London: Fawcett Society).

Finer, Samuel, Hugh Berrington & David Bartholomew (1961) *Backbench Opinion in the House of Commons 1955-9*, (Oxford: Pergamon).

Galligan, Yvonne & Rick Willford (1999) 'Women's political representation in Ireland', in Galligan, Yvonne & Rick Wilford (eds), *Contesting Politics: Women in Ireland, North and South*, (Oxford: Westview).

Guadagnini, Marila (2005) 'Gendering the debate on political representation in Italy: a difficult challenge', in Lovenduski, Joni, Claudie Baudino, Petra Meier & Diane Sainsbury (eds.) (2005) *State Feminism and the Political Representation of Women*, (Cambridge: Cambridge University Press).

Hansard Society Commission (1990) *The Report of the Hansard Society Commission on Women at the Top*, (London: Hansard Society)

Inglehart, Ronald & Pippa Norris (2003) *Rising Tide: Gender Equality and Cultural Change Around the World*, (Cambridge: Cambridge University Press).

Kanter, Rosabeth Moss (1977a) 'Some Effects of Proportions on Group Life', in *American Journal of Sociology* 82:5, 965-90.

Kanter, Rosabeth Moss (1977b) *Men and Women of the Corporation*, (New York: Basic Books).

Karvonen, Lauri & Per Selle (1995) *Women in Nordic Politics: Closing the Gap*, (Aldershot: Dartmouth).

Krook, Mona Lena (2003) 'Gender Quotas: A Framework for Analysis', Paper presented to the General Conference of the European Consortium for Political Research Sept 2003, Marburg.

Lovenduski, Joni (2001), 'Women and Politics', in Pippa Norris (ed.) *Britain Votes 2001*, (Oxford: OUP).

Lovenduski, Joni (1997), 'Gender Politics', in *Parliamentary Affairs*, 50:4, 708-719.

Lovenduski, Joni & Pippa Norris (2003), 'Westminster Women: The Politics of Presence', in *Political Studies*, 51:1, 84-102.

McRae, Susan (1995) *Women at the Top: Progress after five years*, (London: Hansard Society).

Mackay, Fiona (2005) 'The Impact of Devolution on Women's Citizenship in Scotland', summary of paper presented to International Women's Policy Research Conference June 2005, Washington DC.

Mackay, Fiona (2004a) 'Gender and Political Representation in the UK: the State of the 'Discipline', in *British Journal of Politics and International Relations*, 6:1, 99-120.

Mackay, Fiona (2004b) 'Women and Devolution in Scotland', Briefing note prepared for the Scottish Parliament Cross-Party Group on Women and the EOC.

Mackay, Fiona (2004c) 'Women's Representation in Wales and Scotland', in *Contemporary Wales*, 17, 140-161.

Mackay, Fiona (2003) 'Women and the 2003 Elections', in *Scottish Affairs*, 44, 74-90.

Mackay, Fiona (2001) *Love and Politics*, (London: Continuum).

Mackay, Fiona, Elizabeth Meehan Tahyna Donaghy & Paul Chaney (undated) 'Gender and Constitutional Change in Scotland, Northern Ireland and Wales', Unpublished Report.

Mackay, Fiona, Fiona Myers & Alice Brown (2003), 'Towards a New Politics', in Dobrowolsky, Alexandra and Vivien Hart (eds.) *Women Making Constitutions*, (Basingstoke: Palgrave).

Mateo Diaz, Mercedes (2002) *Are Women in Parliament Representing Women?* Doctoral Thesis, (Belgiu, Louvain: Université catholique).

Mazur, Amy (2002) *Theorizing Feminist Policy*, (Oxford: OUP).

Matland, Richard & Kathleen Montgomery (eds.) (2003) *Women's Access to Political Power in Eastern Europe*, (Oxford: Oxford University Press).

Matland, Richard & Donley Studlar (1996) 'The contagion of women candidates in single member district and proportional representation electoral systems: Canada and Norway', in *Journal of Politics*, 58:3.

Meier, Petra (2005) 'The Belgian paradox: inclusion and exclusion of gender issues', in Lovenduski, Joni, Claudie Baudino, Petra Meier & Diane Sainsbury (eds.) (2005) *State Feminism and the Political Representation of Women*, (Cambridge: Cambridge University Press).

Murray, Rainbow, (2005) 'The power of sex and incumbency:a longitudinal study of electoral performance in France', Paper for presentation at the PSA Conference 2005.

Norris, Pippa (1987) *Politics and Sexual Equality: The Comparative Position of Women in Western Democracies*, (Boulder: Lynne Rienner).

Norris, Pippa (1996) 'Women Politicians: Transforming Westminster?', in Lovenduski, Joni & Pippa Norris (eds.) *Women in Politics*, (Oxford: Oxford University Press).

Norris, Pippa (2004) *Electoral Engineering* (Cambridge: Cambridge University Press).

Norris, Pippa & Joni Lovenduski (1995) *Political Recruitment*, (Cambridge: Cambridge University Press).

Norris, Pippa & Joni Lovenduski (1989), 'Women Candidates for Parliament', in *British Journal of Political Science*, 19:1, 106-115.

Norris, Pippa, Joni Lovenduski, & Rosie Campbell (2004) *Gender and Political Participation*, (London: Electoral Commission).

Phillips, Anne (1995) *The Politics of Presence*, (Oxford: Clarendon Press).

Puwar, Nirmal (2004a) *Space Invaders* (Oxford: Berg).

Puwar, Nirmal (2004b), 'Thinking About Making a Difference', in *British Journal of Politics and International Relations*, 6:1, 65-80.

Reingold, Beth (2000) *Representing Women*, (Chapel Hill: University of North Carolina Press).

Ross, Karen (2002) 'Women's Place in 'Male' Space: Gender and Effects in Parliamentary Contexts', in *Parliamentary Affairs*, 55:1, 189-202.

Ross, Karen (2000) *Women at the Top 2000: Cracking the public sector glass ceiling*, (London: Hansard Society & Fawcett Society)

Russell, Meg (2001) *The Women's Representation Bill: Making it Happen*, (London: The Constitution Unit).

Russell, Meg (2000) *Women's Representation in UK Politics: What can be done within the Law?*, (London: The Constitution Unit).

Sapiro, Virgina (1998) 'When are Interests Interesting' in Phillips, Anne (ed), *Feminism and Politics* (Oxford: Oxford University Press), 161-192.

Shaw, Sylvia (2000), 'Language, Gender and Floor Apportionment in Political Debates', in *Discourse and Society*, 11:3, 401-18.

Shepherd-Robinson, Laura and Joni Lovenduski (2002) *Women and Candidate Selection*, (London: Fawcett Society).

Skjeie, Hege (1993) 'Ending the Male Political Hegemony' in Lovenduski, Joni & Pippa Norris (eds.) *Gender and Party Politics*, (London: Sage Publications)

Skjeie, Hege (2002) 'Credo on Difference – Women in Parliament in Norway', http:archive.idea.int/women/parl/studies6a.htm.

Sones, Bonnie, Margaret Moran & Joni Lovenduski (2005) *Women in Parliament, The New Suffragettes*, (Politicos: London).

Squires, Judith & Mark Wickham-Jones (2004) 'New Labour, Gender Mainstreaming and the Women and Equality Unit', in *British Journal of Politics and International Relations*, 6:1, 81-98.

Squires, Judith & Mark Wickham-Jones (2002) 'Mainstreaming in Westminster and Whitehall', in *Parliamentary Affairs*, 55:1, 57-70.

Squires, Judith & Mark Wickham-Jones (2001) *Women in Parliament: A Comparative Analysis*, (Manchester: EOC).

Studlar, Donley T. & Ian McAllister (2002), 'Does a Critical Mass Exist?', in *European Journal of Political Research*, 41:2, 233-53.

Swers, Michele. L. (2002) *The Difference Women Make: The Policy Impact of Women in Congress*, (Chicago: University of Chicago Press).

Tamerius, Karen. L. (1995), 'Sex, Gender, and Leadership in the Representation of Women', in Duerst-Lahti, Georgia & Rita Mae Kelly (eds.) *Gender Power Leadership and Governance*, (USA: The University of Michigan Press).

Thomas, Sue (1994) *How Women Legislate*, (Oxford: Oxford University Press).

Toynbee, Polly & David Walker (2005) *Better or Worse? Has Labour Delivered?*, (Bloomsbury: London).

Vallance, Elizabeth (1979) *Women in the House: A Study of Women in Parliament*, (London: The Athlone Press).

Vallance, Elizabeth & Elizabeth Davies (1986) *Women of Europe: Women MEPs and Equality Policy*, (Cambridge: Cambridge University Press).

Ward, Rachel (2004) 'Gender issues and the Representation of Women in Northern Ireland', in *Irish Political Studies*, 18:2, 1-20.

Ward, Rachel (1997) 'The Northern Ireland Peace Process: A Gender Issue?' in Tonge, John (ed.) *Peace or War? Understanding the Peace Process in Northern Ireland,* (Aldershot: Ashgate).

Weldon, S. Laurel (2002), 'Beyond Bodies: Institutional Sources of Representation for Women in Democratic Policymaking', in *The Journal of Politics*, 64:4, 1153-74.

Women and Work Commission (2005) *A Fair Deal for Women in the Workplace: An Interim Statement*, www.womenandequalityunit.gov.uk/women_work_commission.

Yoder, Janice (1991) 'Rethinking Tokenism: Looking Beyond Numbers', *in Gender and Society*, 5, 178-192.